Apple Training Series

GarageBand '09

Mary Plummer

Apple
Certified

Apple Training Series: GarageBand '09
Mary Plummer
Copyright © 2009 by Mary Plummer

Published by Peachpit Press. For information on Peachpit Press books, contact:

Peachpit Press
1249 Eighth Street
Berkeley, CA 94710
(510) 524-2178
Fax: (510) 524-2221
http://www.peachpit.com
To report errors, please send a note to errata@peachpit.com
Peachpit Press is a division of Pearson Education

Apple Series Editor: Serena Herr
Project Editor: Stephen Nathans-Kelly
Production Coordinator: Kim Wimpsett
Technical Editor: Charlie Miller
Technical Reviewer: Brendan Boykin
Copy Editor: Karen Seriguchi
Proofer: Karen Seriguchi
Compositor: Chris Gillespie, Happenstance Type-O-Rama
Media Producer: Eric Geoffroy
Indexer: Jack Lewis
Cover Illustration: Kent Oberheu
Cover Production: Happenstance Type-O-Rama

ISBN-13: 978-0-321-64852-5
ISBN-10: 0-321-64852-8
9 8 7 6 5 4 3 2 1
Printed and bound in the United States of America

Contents at a Glance

Table of Contents

Getting Started

Welcome to the official training course for GarageBand '09, Apple's dynamic music recording and arranging software. This is a guide to recording and arranging songs, creating podcasts, adding music and sound effects to your movies, mixing music, creating your own instrument recordings, and working with the library of more than 1,000 royalty-free Apple Loops that are included with the software. You'll also explore new GarageBand '09 features like the Learn to Play lessons, and you'll perform with virtual musicians onstage with Magic GarageBand Jam.

Apple Training Series: GarageBand '09 is based on the premise that a training book should go beyond a basic tour of an application. It provides you with practical techniques that you will use on a daily basis to add professional-quality music and sound effects to your projects.

Whether you're a seasoned composer or have never written a piece of music before, you'll learn how to use GarageBand for a variety of real-world scenarios, including recording, arranging, and mixing music from scratch. You'll work with Real Instruments, MIDI Software Instruments, and prerecorded Apple Loops to edit music and add effects that sweeten your finished projects. Finally, you'll prepare your projects for iTunes and explore sharing your finished projects with other iLife applications.

The Methodology

This book emphasizes hands-on training. Each exercise is designed to help you learn the application as you use it, starting with the basic interface and moving on to advanced music editing, arranging, and mixing techniques.

If you're new to GarageBand, it will be helpful for you to start at the beginning and progress through each lesson in order, since each lesson builds on information learned in the previous ones. If you're already familiar with GarageBand, you can start with any section and focus on that topic.

Course Structure

Each of the eight lessons in this book focuses on a different aspect of creating projects with GarageBand '09. Each lesson expands on the basic concepts of the program, giving you the tools to use GarageBand for your own projects.

The lessons in this book can be informally divided into five sections:

▶ Lessons 1–2: Learning to play an instrument and jamming with virtual musicians onstage.

▶ Lessons 3–5: Recording and arranging music. You'll work with GarageBand regions, such as Software Instruments, Real Instruments, and Apple Loops, and use project presets to record original music, arrange musical parts and sound effects to score a movie, and create two types of ringtones.

▶ Lesson 6: Mixing and adding effects to complete a project.

▶ Lesson 7: Creating original podcasts.

▶ Lesson 8: Preparing songs for iTunes, and exporting projects to other applications.

At the end of the book, we've included an appendix. "Bonus Lessons and Materials" offers exercises in working with loops and exporting selected tracks. It also gives tips on some of the application preferences that will minimize the processor load as you work in GarageBand. The final section takes you on a tour of available Jam Packs and helps you expand the horizons of your musical creations.

System Requirements

This book is written for GarageBand '09, part of the iLife '09 suite of products that come free with any new Macintosh computer. If you have an older version of iLife, you'll need to upgrade to the current version of iLife to follow along with every lesson. The upgrade can be purchased online at www.apple.com or from any store that sells Apple software.

Before you begin the lessons in this book, you should have a working knowledge of your Mac and its operating system. You don't need to be an expert, but you do need to know how to use the mouse and standard menus and commands, and how to open, save, and close files. You should have a working understanding of how OS X helps organize files on your computer, and you should also be comfortable opening applications (from the Dock or at least the Applications folder). If you need to review any of these techniques, see the printed or online documentation that came with your computer.

For a list of the minimum system requirements for GarageBand '09, please refer to the Apple website at www.apple.com/ilife/systemrequirements.html.

Hardware Compatibility

GarageBand '09 can operate with any Core Audio–compliant or Core MIDI–compliant audio interface, USB MIDI interface, or even a microphone, keyboard, or guitar with the correct adapter. You may need to install additional drivers from the manufacturer of the audio interface in order to provide full Mac OS X support.

For a list of supported audio and MIDI interfaces that work with GarageBand, see the GarageBand website at www.apple.com/ilife/garageband.

Installing GarageBand

To install GarageBand, double-click the GarageBand installer and follow the instructions that appear.

If you see a message that you do not have sufficient privileges to install this software, click the lock icon in the installer window and enter an administrator name and password. The administrators of your computer are shown in the Accounts pane of System Preferences.

The installer places the Apple Loops library and the index to the loops library in the Library/Audio folder of your home folder, and it places the instrument library in the Library/Application Support/GarageBand folder of your home folder. Do not move these items from their default locations.

Copying the Lesson Files

This book includes an *ATS_GarageBand09* DVD, which contains all the files you'll need to complete the lessons. Inside the GarageBand09_Book_Files folder are Lesson subfolders organized by lesson number. Within each numbered Lesson subfolder, you will find projects for each exercise.

When you install these files on your computer, it's important to keep all of the numbered Lesson subfolders together in the main GarageBand09_Book_Files folder on your hard disk. If you copy the GarageBand09_Book_Files folder directly from the DVD to your hard disk, you should not need to reconnect any media files or have problems opening projects.

Installing the Lesson Files

1   Put the *ATS_GarageBand09* DVD into your computer's DVD drive.

2   Double-click to open the DVD and drag the GarageBand09_Book_Files folder from the DVD to your computer's desktop.

3   To begin each lesson, open GarageBand. Then follow the instructions in the exercises to open the project files for that lesson.

About Apple Training and Certification

Apple Training Series: GarageBand '09 is part of the official training series for Apple applications, developed by experts in the field and certified by Apple. The lessons are designed to let you learn at your own pace. If you follow the book from start to finish, or at least complete the lessons in each section con-secutively, you will build on what you learned in previous lessons.

Apple Certification offers Associate-level certification for the iLife '09 product suite. Professionals, educators, and students can earn Apple Certified Associate status to validate entry-level skills in the Apple digital lifestyle applications. As a special offer, this Apple Pro Training Series book includes a discount code that lets you take the certification exam online for $45 (a $65 value). While this book only partially prepares you for this exam, you can use the free Skills Assessment Guide at http://training.apple.com/certification/associate to deter-mine whether you are ready to take this exam. Details appear on the DVD.

For those who prefer to learn in an instructor-led setting, Apple also offers training courses that lead to certification at Apple Authorized Training Centers worldwide in iLife, iWork, Mac OS X, Mac OS X Server, and Apple's Pro appli-cations. Taught by Apple Certified Trainers, these courses balance concepts and lectures with hands-on labs and exercises.

To learn more about Apple Training and Certification, or to find an Authorized Training Center near you, go to http://training.apple.com.

Resources

Apple Training Series: GarageBand '09 is not intended to be a comprehensive reference manual, nor does it replace the documentation that comes with the application. Rather, the book is designed to be used in conjunction with other reference guides. These resources include:

▶ Companion Peachpit website: As GarageBand '09 is updated, Peachpit may choose to update lessons as necessary. Please check www.peachpit .com/ats.GarageBand09.

▶ Apple's website: www.apple.com.

▶ *Apple Training Series: iLife '09* is an excellent companion to this book. Learn how to use the other iLife applications in addition to GarageBand.

1

Lesson Files	No files for this lesson
Time	This lesson takes approximately 30 minutes to complete.
Goals	Connect instruments to the computer
	Explore the Learn to Play interface
	Customize the Learn to Play lesson window
	Download additional Learn to Play lessons

Learning to Play Music with GarageBand

Whether you're an accomplished musician or a hobbyist, or simply someone who enjoys other people's music, GarageBand can help you take your musical aspirations to the next level—no experience required!

GarageBand '09 has evolved into a fully functional musician's workshop with all of the tools you need to learn, record, compose, produce, mix, and share your music.

This lesson focuses on the Learn to Play lessons that can teach you to play either guitar or piano.

If you don't have an instrument at this time, feel free to read along with the lesson to get an idea of how GarageBand Learn to Play lessons work.

Opening GarageBand

In this section, you're going to open GarageBand and take a look at the various options available for learning, playing, composing, and recording music.

1   Click the GarageBand icon in the Dock to open it.

The GarageBand welcome screen opens.

This window includes links to the GarageBand video tutorials, as well as information on getting hands-on help.

For now let's close the window and move on to the actual interface.

TIP▶ If you don't care to see the welcome screen every time that you open GarageBand, deselect the checkbox in the lower-left corner of the window before closing it.

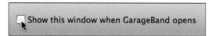

2   Click the Close button (x) to dismiss the welcome screen.

The New Project dialog appears, with buttons for all of the different project types, including New Project, Magic GarageBand, and iPhone Ringtone.

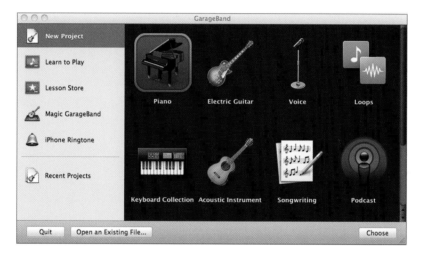

3   Click the New Project button to see a list of project templates appear in the main area of the window. Templates are included for piano, electric guitar, voice, loops, keyboards, acoustic instruments, songwriting, podcast, and movie scoring.

You'll work more with the project templates in several lessons later in this book. For now, you can leave the New Project dialog open while you connect your instrument in the next section.

Connecting Musical Instruments to Your Computer

There are two types of musical instruments: electric and acoustic. An electric instrument has a built-in interface to output its sound, but an acoustic instrument needs a microphone to record its sound.

Electric instruments include electric guitars, electric keyboards, and electric bass. You can connect an electric instrument directly to your computer's audio-in port, if your computer has one. The computer audio-in port is a ⅛ -inch mini input, so you'll need an adapter or cable to convert the ¼ -inch output from your instrument to the ⅛ -inch audio-in port (mini input) on the computer.

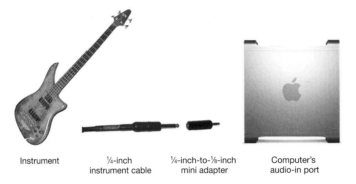

| Instrument | ¼-inch instrument cable | ¼-inch-to-⅛-inch mini adapter | Computer's audio-in port |

To record an acoustic instrument or vocals, you can connect a microphone to your computer through the audio-in port. Mac Pro computers also include optical digital audio in/out ports for higher-end audio recording equipment.

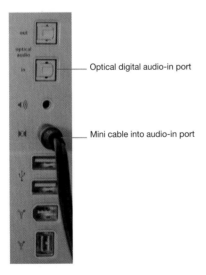

Optical digital audio-in port

Mini cable into audio-in port

You can also connect an audio interface to your computer and then connect your microphone or instruments to the audio interface. There is a wide range of audio interfaces and compatible formats, including USB, FireWire, PCI, and

PC cards. With the addition of an audio interface, GarageBand allows you to record up to eight Real Instrument tracks and one Software Instrument track simultaneously. An audio mixer or console will also record more than one instrument or microphone at once, but it will mix all the inputs into only one stereo track.

Make sure that whatever audio interface you use is compatible with Mac OS X 10.5.6 or later (for GarageBand '09) and that your computer supports the format used by the interface. Your interface documents should state whether it's compatible with your Mac.

To set up recording using your Mac's built-in port, do the following:

1   Choose System Preferences > Sound > Input and select Line In > Audio line-in port as your sound input device.

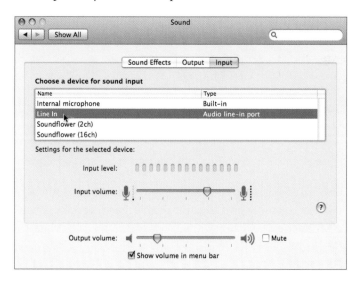

2   Play your instrument and adjust the Input volume slider until you achieve a good level without peaking/clipping.

Once you've finished connecting your instrument, you can continue to the next sections to explore the Learn to Play exercises for guitar and piano, or move on to Lesson 2, "Jamming with a Virtual Band," to play along with virtual musicians.

Connecting a MIDI Instrument to Your Computer

MIDI stands for Musical Instrument Digital Interface. It's an industry standard that allows devices such as synthesizers and computers to communicate with each other.

A USB MIDI keyboard or other MIDI controller connects directly to the computer and to the keyboard with a USB cable.

To connect a USB MIDI keyboard to the computer, simply plug it into a spare USB port. To connect a standard MIDI controller such as a keyboard, you'll need a USB-to-MIDI interface. Connect the keyboard to the MIDI interface device using standard MIDI cables. Then connect the interface to your computer using the USB cable. Carefully read the instructions that come with the keyboard and MIDI interface, and be sure to install all of the necessary drivers.

> **MORE INFO** ▶ For more information about GarageBand accessories, including MIDI keyboards, USB keyboards, or MIDI interfaces, visit Apple's website.

Learning to Play Guitar or Piano

Are you one of the millions of people who say they wish they had learned how to play piano or guitar when they had the chance? Well, if you have a Mac, a guitar, a piano or MIDI keyboard, and GarageBand '09, this is your chance! Many of you already have an instrument in the house (or garage or attic, collecting dust), and if not, you probably know someone who will lend you one.

GarageBand's new Learn to Play lessons are perfect for anyone who is ready to start taking lessons, or for someone who took lessons a long time ago and needs a refresher, or even for a student who is currently taking lessons and would like some personal tutoring at home.

Rather than guide you through an entire basic lesson, the next few exercises are designed to introduce you to the Learn to Play lessons interface, as well as the recording and customizable features, so that when you're ready to sit down for a full Learn to Play lesson you'll be ready to rock and roll (literally).

Taking a Guitar or Piano Lesson

This section will cover the features of both the Intro to Guitar and Intro to Piano Learn to Play lessons. If you have an instrument connected to the computer, follow along with the steps appropriate for that instrument. Most of the steps will be the same for both guitar and piano lessons.

GarageBand '09 includes nine free basic lessons for both guitar and piano. The first lesson for both instruments is automatically installed on your computer when you install iLife '09.

You don't need to have a guitar or piano handy to follow along with this exercise. When you're ready to take an actual Learn to Play lesson, you'll need to connect your instrument to the computer to fully explore interactive features such as tuning and recording your practice.

You open the first Learn to Play lessons from the New Project dialog.

> **NOTE** ▶ If you don't want to learn about the Learn to Play lessons at this time, feel free to jump to Lesson 2, "Jamming with a Virtual Band."

1   Open GarageBand and click Learn to Play in the list of project types in the New Project dialog.

2   Select either Piano Lesson 1 or Guitar Lesson 1, then click Choose or press Return.

The screen fades out and the lesson opens.

NOTE ▶ You can also open a Learn to Play lesson by double-clicking a lesson icon on the GarageBand Project window.

Exploring the Interface

Now that the Intro to Guitar or Intro to Piano lesson is open, you can see the default interface. The interface includes a video area in the upper part of the screen and an animated instrument in the lower part of the screen. Transport controls are located in the dark gray control bar at the bottom of the screen. You can use these controls to record, play/pause, or repeat parts of the lesson.

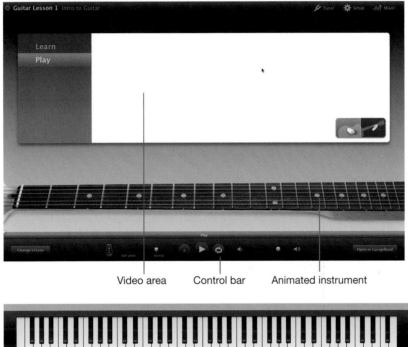

Video area   Control bar   Animated instrument

Each lesson includes at least two chapters; in these examples the chapters explain how you can Learn (take a lesson) or Play (watch and listen to the instructor playing the lesson song). It's a good idea to start with the Play chapter to familiarize yourself with the music that you'll be learning during the lesson. In this case, the music is simply the strumming of an E chord.

Let's play the music and explore some of the different controls to adjust the playback while the music and video play.

1   Double-click the Play Chapter button in the upper-left corner of the video area.

The music starts and the video area shows two views of the instructor playing the guitar or piano.

NOTE ▶ To exit the lesson at any time, click the X (close button) in the upper-left corner of the screen.

2   Move the pointer to the empty gray space below the video area to see the entire video, without any overlays.

The left side of the video area will always show the instructor and the full guitar or piano. For the guitar lessons the right side can show either the guitar with the instructor's hands only, or the top of the fretboard.

3   If you're following the guitar lesson, move the pointer to the lower-right corner of the video area and click back and forth between the two view buttons to change views of the guitar.

4   Click the Play button in the control bar, or press the Spacebar to pause playback.

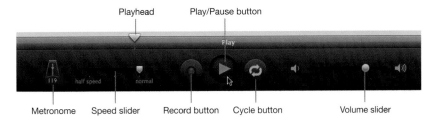

5   While playback is stopped, drag the playhead left or right to move to a point earlier or later in the song.

6   Press the Right Arrow or Left Arrow key to move the playhead incrementally left or right.

7   Press Return to move the playhead to the beginning of the song.

8   Press the Spacebar, or click the Play button to start playback again.

NOTE ▶ The volume slider in the lesson interface works independently of the volume controls for your Mac, and controls only the volume level of the lesson playback. You can adjust the levels within the lesson interface as needed. If you don't hear anything at all, check to make sure that your computer volume levels are not muted or set too low.

9   Click the Metronome button to turn on the click track while the music plays. Feel free to click the Metronome button again to turn off the metronome whenever you like.

10 Drag the Speed slider to the left to slow down the tempo (speed) of the music playback.

When you adjust the playback speed for the first time, a warning dialog appears to tell you that slowing down the speed will mute the instructor's voice. If you don't want to see this warning every time you adjust the speed, select the "Don't show again" checkbox.

11 Click OK to close the dialog and slow down the playback tempo.

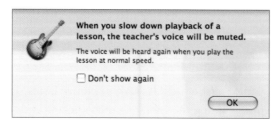

12 Experiment with the different controls, then click the Play button or press the Spacebar to stop playback. Be sure to return the Speed slider to the normal (full right) position.

Now that you're familiar with some of the different playback options and controls, let's move on to the lesson.

13 Double-click the word *Learn* in the upper-left corner of the video area to switch to the lesson interface.

The lesson starts with an introduction of the instructor, Tim.

14 Stop playback.

You can follow the entire lesson shortly if you'd like. But first, let's take a few minutes to learn how to navigate between sections, and explore some of the customizing features available to enhance your lesson experience.

Navigating Between Lesson Sections

Each Learn to Play lesson comes with at least two chapters. The sections are listed in order along the timeline above the transport controls.

As you can see, the Intro to Guitar lesson includes seven sections: Learn, Acoustic Guitar, Electric Guitar, Holding the Guitar, Tuning, Picking and Strumming, and Strumming an E Chord.

The Intro to Piano lesson includes eight sections: Learn, Black and White Keys, Playing Position, Sustain Pedal, Chords, Chord Progressions, Rhythm, and Next Steps.

The playback controls and keyboard shortcuts work the same for the Learn interface as they did in the Play interface. The difference is the ability to jump around from section to section, or cycle (loop) a specific section.

1   Start playback of the lesson.

2   Click any of the section titles listed in the timeline to jump to the beginning of that section.

3   Click the Cycle button in the Control bar to cycle (repeat/loop) the selected section.

The selected section title turns yellow to indicate that a cycle region has been created for that section. It will cycle (repeat) continuously until playback is stopped, another section is selected, or the Cycle button is turned off.

NOTE ▶ If all of the section titles turn yellow at once, the entire lesson is included in the cycle region. Click any specific section title to limit the cycle region to the selected section.

4   Turn off the Cycle button and pause playback.

Now that you've learned how to select, navigate, and cycle through sections within the lesson, let's move on to some of the cool customizing features.

Customizing the Lesson Workspace

One of most helpful features for taking a lesson is the ability to customize the lesson's appearance at any time to suit your specific needs. For example, you can show or hide the animated instrument, or change the notation view. For guitar lessons you can show a notation view between the video area and the animated fretboard, or hide the animated fretboard and view only the notation with the video.

All of the customizing choices are available in the setup window that can be accessed via the Setup button near the upper-right corner of the screen.

1   Click the Setup button.

The setup window appears with choices for notation and appearance.

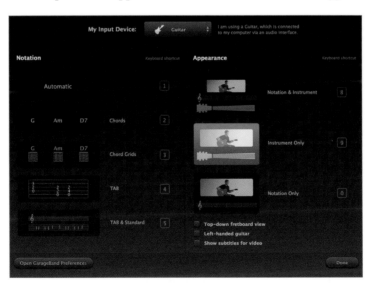

Notice the numeric keyboard shortcut next to each choice. These can be used to change the lesson appearance instantly without interrupting playback.

2   For the guitar lesson, select TAB & Standard under the Notation column.

This view includes a combination of two common types of guitar notation.

For the piano lesson, select Both Hands under the Notation column.

NOTE ▶ In Automatic view, the notation appearance will change automatically, depending on what is being presented in the lesson. For the guitar lesson, because this particular lesson includes only basic picking and strumming, Automatic view actually hides the notation for most of the lesson.

3   Select Notation & Instrument under the Appearance column.

4   Click Done to return to the lesson.

5   For the guitar lesson, play the Picking and Strumming section.

6   For the piano lesson, play the Chord Progressions section.

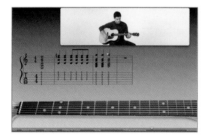 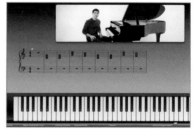

Notation appears in the middle of the screen whenever the instructor plays the guitar or piano.

Notice that the animated instrument also shows which notes are played in unison with the notation.

7   Press the numeric keys 2 through 5 to alternate notation between chord names; chord fingering grids (guitar) or left hand only (piano); tablature (guitar) or right hand only (piano); and tablature and standard notation (guitar) or both hands (piano). Press keys 8, 9, and 0 to change the appearance between notation and animated instrument; animated instrument only; and notation only. Press 1 for Automatic view. When you're finished experimenting with the different views, stop the lesson playback.

NOTE ▶ The setup window also includes checkboxes to select views for a left-handed guitar, top-down fretboard, and subtitles for the video. You can also use the My Input Device menu at the top of the setup window to change your guitar input settings for the lesson.

Tuning and Recording During a Lesson

In addition to taking a lesson, you can also tune your guitar and record your practice during the lesson. Because both of these features require a guitar or keyboard that is connected to the computer, they won't be included as exercises in this lesson.

The Tuner button is located next to the Setup button near the upper-right corner of the screen.

To tune your guitar, simply click the Tuner button and play the string that you want to tune. The visual tuner works the same as most professional guitar tuners.

To record your practice, move the playhead to the place where you want to start recording, click the Record button in the control bar, and play your guitar. Click the Play button when you're finished. For a guitar recording, a purple Real Instrument region appears below the playhead; for a piano recording, you'll see a green Software Instrument region. You'll learn more about the different types of regions in the next lesson.

Recording   Finished region

TIP ▶ To record multiple takes, turn on the Cycle button, and select the section you want to record. Record as many takes as you want; when you stop recording a number appears indicating the number of takes. You can click the take number in the upper-left corner of the purple recording region to choose a different take. You'll learn more about multiple-take recording in Lesson 3, "Recording Music in GarageBand."

Changing a Lesson Mix

Because practice, practice, and more practice is an important part of any successful music lesson, you may want to adjust the lesson mix as you progress to better suit your practice needs. For example, you would probably grow tired of the instructor's voice saying the same thing over and over when all you want to focus on is the sound of his guitar or piano, or perhaps the sound of your own instrument. Let's take a look at the lesson mixer and see how to change the lesson mix.

1   Click the Mixer button, located in the upper-right corner of the screen.

The mixer appears as an overlay over the lesson window.

Each track includes a Mute button to silence a track, a Solo button to play only that track, and a volume slider to adjust the track's volume.

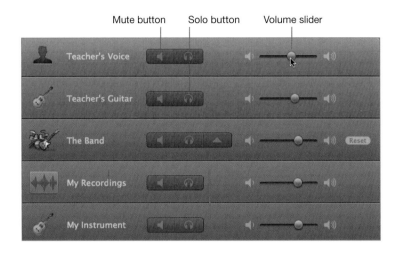

Mute button   Solo button   Volume slider

NOTE ▶ The My Recordings track appears only if you've recorded your instrument with the lesson.

2 For the guitar lesson, play the Picking and Strumming section.

3 For the piano lesson, play the Chord Progressions section.

   While the lesson plays, click the Mute button on the Teacher's Voice track to mute the track.

   The mixer buttons, like other controls within GarageBand, turn blue to indicate that they're on.

4 Click the Mute button again to unmute the track.

5 Experiment with the different mixer controls. When you're finished, click the Mixer button to hide the mixer.

6 Click the X (close) button in the upper-left corner of the lesson window to close the lesson.

That's it. Now you know your way around a Learn to Play lesson.

Downloading Additional Learn to Play Lessons

So you've finished the first Learn to Play lesson. Are you ready for more? GarageBand now includes eight more Learn to Play basic guitar or piano lessons that you can download right to your computer—and they're free!

The additional Learn to Play guitar lessons are as follows:

▶   Guitar Lesson 2   Chords – G, C

▶   Guitar Lesson 3   Chords – A, D

▶   Guitar Lesson 4   Minor Chords

▶   Guitar Lesson 5   Single Note Melodies

▶   Guitar Lesson 6   Power Chords

▶   Guitar Lesson 7   Major Barre Chords

▶   Guitar Lesson 8   Minor Barre Chords

▶   Guitar Lesson 9   Blues Lead

The additional Learn to Play piano lessons are as follows:

▶   Piano Lesson 2   Right Hand

▶   Piano Lesson 3   Left Hand

▶   Piano Lesson 4   Rhythm

▶   Piano Lesson 5   Sharps and Flats

▶   Piano Lesson 6   Rhythmic Accents

▶   Piano Lesson 7   Major and Minor Chords

▶   Piano Lesson 8   Scales

▶   Piano Lesson 9   Playing the Blues

To download your next lesson, you'll need to choose it from the Lesson Store.

NOTE ▶ If you don't want to download another lesson, you can still follow along with this exercise; just don't click the Download button when prompted to do so.

1   Click the Lesson Store in the New Project dialog.

The Learn to Play piano and guitar lessons are listed.

2 Click the Basic Lessons button at the top of the dialog, if it isn't already selected.

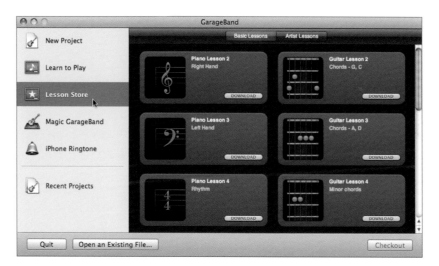

3 Click the Download button on the specific lesson that you'd like to download.

A dialog appears confirming the download.

4   Click Download in the dialog to begin the download.

The lesson is downloaded to your computer and an icon for the lesson appears in the Learn to Play lessons list in the New Project dialog.

Taking an Artist Lesson

If your piano and guitar skills have grown beyond the basic lessons, you're ready to learn from the pros. Artist Lessons use the same interface as the basic Learn to Play lessons, with the advantage that your instructor is the actual recording artist who made the music a hit. Want to learn "Roxanne" from Sting, "Thinking About You" from Norah Jones, or "Proud Mary" from John Fogerty? You can do it in GarageBand. The Artist Lessons also include personal stories told by the artists about their songs.

These more advanced lessons are available for purchase from the Lesson Store.

To purchase an Artist Lesson, click the Lesson Store button in the New Project dialog, then click the Artist Lessons button to see the list. From there you can view the different choices and click Add to Cart; then follow the instructions to purchase and download the lesson.

Lesson Review

1. Which instruments have Learn to Play lessons included with GarageBand?

2. How do you download additional lessons?

3. Do you have to have an instrument connected to the computer to take a Learn to Play lesson?

Answers

1. GarageBand includes Learn to Play lessons for both piano and guitar.

2. You click the Lesson Store button on the New Project dialog, then choose the lesson that you want to download.

3. You can take a Learn to Play lesson with or without an instrument; however, having a guitar or keyboard connected to the computer allows you to tune (for guitars) and play along with the instructor during the lesson.

2

Lesson Files	GarageBand09_Book_Files > Lesson_02 > Magic Rock Song
Time	This lesson takes approximately 30 minutes to complete.
Goals	Choose a Magic GarageBand Jam genre
	Audition and select instrument parts
	Work with the mixer during an audition
	Select and customize your instrument part
	Record a keyboard part using Musical Typing
	Open and save a finished song

Jamming with a Virtual Band

One of the greatest pleasures of being a musician is performing with a band onstage in front of a huge crowd of screaming fans. That might not be a reality for everyone, but playing along with GarageBand's virtual musicians is a great way to practice, create music quickly, play and record original riffs, or just jam along and enjoy the process (screaming fans optional). Magic GarageBand Jam puts you at center stage as the leader of a virtual band and offers nine genres of music to choose from.

Whether you're a professional musician, or have just finished your Learn to Play lessons, Magic GarageBand Jam offers a flexible performance experience to take your musical skills to the next level.

The next series of exercises will lead you through a hands-on tour of Magic GarageBand Jam. Along the way you'll choose a genre, audition musicians, select your own instrument, record a simple part, and finally open and save the finished song in GarageBand.

Let's get started.

Selecting a Music Genre

Magic GarageBand Jam offers nine music genres to choose from: blues, rock, jazz, country, reggae, funk, Latin, roots rock, and slow blues.

You can preview the various genres right in the New Project dialog.

1   Open GarageBand. If GarageBand is already open, choose File > New.

2   In the New Project dialog, click the Magic GarageBand button.

An icon for each of the nine genres appears in the project list. To preview a genre, simply move your pointer over a genre icon until you see the preview overlay appear. Then click the small Play Preview button.

3   Move your pointer over the Blues icon and click the Play Preview button to hear the blues song. Click the button again to stop the preview.

TIP You can use your computer volume level controls to adjust the preview volume levels.

4   Preview some of the different genres to hear the variety of music that you can jam along with in Magic GarageBand Jam.

For this lesson, let's use the Rock genre.

5   Double-click the Rock genre icon to open that project.

After a moment the Magic GarageBand stage appears along with the default instruments used in the song.

Navigating and Controlling Playback

Now that you've opened a Magic GarageBand project, it's a good idea to learn how to navigate your way around a song and to control playback.

If you already completed the Learn to Play exercises in Lesson 1, you'll see some familiar features in the control bar at the bottom of the window. If you skipped ahead to this lesson, no problem; you'll be acquainted with the controls soon.

1   Click the Play button in the control bar to play the song.

The music plays in its default arrangement. You can use the volume slider if you need to increase the song's volume temporarily.

2   Press the Spacebar to pause playback.

3   Press Return to move the playhead back to the beginning of the song.

Each Magic GarageBand song includes an intro, two verses, a chorus, and an ending. You can quickly navigate to the beginning of one of these sections by clicking the corresponding part above the control bar.

4   Click Verse 1 to select that section of the song.

The selected section turns yellow, and the playhead jumps to the beginning of that section.

5   Press the Spacebar or click the Play button to start playback again.

Notice that this time the playback includes only the selected snippet of the song. This feature comes in really handy if you want to practice or play along with just one part of the song at a time.

6   Click the Snippet/Entire Song switch to set it back to Entire Song and pause playback.

The yellow highlighted section of the song disappears, and the entire song plays again.

You can also play the project full screen by clicking the small View button in the lower-right corner of the stage.

You can click the View button again at any time to return to the window view.

NOTE ▶ If you're using the full-screen view, you can click the X (close button) in the upper-left corner of the screen to close Magic GarageBand at any time.

Auditioning Virtual Musicians (Instrument Parts)

Now that you've opened the song and know how to control playback, you can audition the different instrument parts.

Each Magic GarageBand song includes Guitar, Bass, Drums, Keyboard and Melody instruments, and a place for you (My Instrument) at the center of the stage. As the leader of the virtual band, you decide which musicians get to play, as well as controlling the instrument and feeling of the part.

The good news is that your job is much easier than auditioning musicians in the real world. In Magic GarageBand the virtual musicians are very professional, which means you don't have to deal with egos, tardiness, attitude, or poor playing. Instead, you can focus on choosing the right parts for your unique version of the song—there are more than 3,000 possible combinations of sounds for each genre.

1   Move the pointer over each instrument on the stage to see the name of each instrument part.

The spotlight illuminates whichever instrument you roll the pointer over, and the name of the instrument or part appears.

2 Click the guitar on the left side of the stage to select that instrument part.

The instrument list below the stage changes to show the choices for the song's guitar part. In this case, there are seven guitar styles from which to choose: Jangle, Strumming, Honky Tonk, Punk, Windmills, Big Stack, and Glam.

The No Instrument choice on the far right of the instrument list is also available if you don't want to include a particular instrument in the song at all.

If you aren't familiar with these different guitar styles, no problem. You can simply change them while the song is playing to hear how they change the feel and sound of the song.

TIP It's a good idea to audition instruments against one section (snippet) of the song, such as the verse or chorus, so that you hear all of the different choices in the same context.

3 Play the song, and click Verse 1 to loop playback of that section (snippet) of the song.

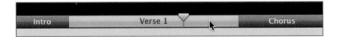

4 Click each of the guitar sounds in the list to audition them with the first
verse of the song.

When you change instrument sounds, the new instrument (virtual musician) needs to wait until the next measure to jump in—so be sure to give
each guitar a chance to play before moving on to the next one.

You should notice a clear difference in the sound of the guitars.

NOTE ▶ GarageBand comes with an awesome set of guitar amps and
stompbox effects to create these sounds—and more—with your own
guitar recordings.

5 Choose your favorite guitar sound.

If you're having trouble deciding, try the Big Stack for a nice over-the-
top, heavy electric guitar with plenty of effects. I like this one because it
reminds me of the "check out my big amp and effects" sound of the guitars in every band I played keyboards for in high school and college (way
back in the '80s, long before GarageBand, though we did practice and
record music in the garage).

6 Stop playback, if you haven't already.

Now that you know how to audition and select different instrument parts,
let's take a look at some additional mixing features that you can use to make
choosing instrument parts even easier.

Mixing Instruments in Magic GarageBand

Auditioning instruments while listening to the other parts works well to get
a feel for how the part fits with the overall sound. However, sometimes you
may want to solo or mute a particular instrument before you make your final
decision.

Each instrument part includes a mixer that allows you to control the volume
of that instrument in the overall mix, as well as solo and mute controls.

In this exercise you'll use the mixer to help with the audition of the bass part.

1   Click the bass to select that instrument.

2   Click the disclosure triangle on the left side of the Bass overlay to show the mixer.

3   Start playback. Feel free to choose a different part of the song for the bass audition.

4   Click the Solo button to isolate the sound of the bass.

You should hear only the sound of the bass instrument. This is a great way to hear the part clearly.

5   Choose a different bass instrument from the instrument list and listen to it.

6   Click the Solo button again to unsolo the new part.

7 Toggle the Solo button on and off as needed while you audition the remaining bass parts. Select different parts of the song to hear the bass in the intro, chorus, verses, and ending. Stop playback when you're happy with your bass selection.

If can't decide on a bass part, try the Driving bass. It has a nice presence without overshadowing the Big Stack guitar.

The good news is that there is no right or wrong choice. All of the parts sound great; that is part of the "magic" of Magic GarageBand Jam.

TIP ▶ A fast way to find a new combination of instrument parts is to click an empty part of the stage, then click the Shuffle Instruments button. *Voila!* Now the song has a fresh sound with a different set of instruments.

Project Practice

Take a few minutes to practice what you've learned so far, and select new instruments for the drums, keyboard, and melody parts. If you like the way the song sounds as is, you can leave the default instruments and move on to the next section.

NOTE ▶ Magic GarageBand Jam automatically saves your changes to the song as you go. If you need to close the project and come back to it later, just double-click the Rock genre icon from the Magic GarageBand Jam genre list and it will open exactly the way you left it.

Setting Up Your Instrument

Now that the musicians and instruments have been selected, the last step is to choose the instrument that you'll play. Once you've set up your own instrument, you can play along and even record your part.

1 Click the grand piano labeled My Instrument located at the center of the stage.

The default instrument for the Rock genre is a grand piano.

2 Click the My Instrument menu to see the choices of instruments that you can use and have connected to the computer.

Your choices are as follows:

▶ **Keyboard** is for using a MIDI instrument such as a piano or organ. If you don't have an external MIDI instrument, you can also play along using your computer's keyboard.

▶ **Guitar** is for using an instrument such as a guitar or bass that is connected through the audio-in port or another approved audio interface. This could also include a microphone that you're using to record vocals or other acoustic instruments.

▶ **Internal Mic** allows you to record your voice or another instrument such as a harmonica using the computer's built-in mic.

For this exercise let's use the Keyboard setting and play a part using the computer keyboard.

3 Choose Keyboard from the My Instrument menu, if it isn't already selected.

Magic GarageBand Jam includes three default keyboard choices: Grand Piano, Electric Piano, and Arena Run.

4   Choose the Grand Piano instrument if it isn't already selected.

    To play this instrument using your computer keyboard, you need to turn on Musical Typing.

5   Click the Tuner button to turn on Musical Typing.

The Musical Typing keyboard appears below the stage. You can click the notes on the Musical Typing keyboard to play them, or type the corresponding notes on your computer keyboard. Notice that the Tab key works as a sustain pedal, and the Z and X keys will change the octave lower and higher, respectively.

6   Start playback and play a few notes on your computer keyboard to hear how they sound. Don't worry if they aren't the right notes. This exercise is just to illustrate how Musical Typing works. When you're finished jamming, stop playback.

NOTE ▶ The My Instrument menu includes Monitor Off and Monitor On choices. If you don't need to hear your instrument through the computer speakers or headphones, you can choose Monitor Off. This may be handy if you want to monitor (listen to) the other instruments through your headphones, because you can hear your instrument (such as vocals or acoustic guitar) without adding it to the mix. The Monitor Off setting is also a good way to avoid feedback if your live mic is too close to the speakers. The default setting is Monitor On.

Adding an Instrument

The other instruments in your song are limited to specific styles, but your instrument part has an advantage in that you can choose from any sound available in GarageBand. In this exercise, you'll customize the choice and add a new sound that you can play on your computer keyboard or with an external MIDI keyboard.

1   Click the Tuner button again to see the My Instrument keyboard instrument list.

2   Click the Customize button.

The Instrument menu appears, showing all of the available Pianos and Keyboards instruments. Your instrument list may have fewer instruments than the one shown, which includes sounds from Jam Pack: World Music.

For this exercise, let's choose an interesting synth pad to add some electronic '80s texture to this rock song.

3   Click the Pianos and Keyboards menu header to see a full list of Software Instrument categories.

4   Choose Synth Pads from the Instrument menu.

5   Choose Falling Star from the Synth Pads instrument list. Then click Done
to hide the Instrument menu.

The Customize button is replaced by the Falling Star instrument in the list.

NOTE ► You can click the Info button (the circled "i") in the upper-right
corner of the Falling Star icon to show the Instrument menu and choose a
different customized instrument.

6   Click the Tuner button to turn on Musical Typing and play a few notes
along with the song. When you're finished, stop playback.

The Falling Star sound is easy to work with—even if you aren't a musician.
Sure, it isn't a very good choice for showing off your finger work or composing a keyboard solo, but it's perfect for adding a little excitement to the
intro and ending of the song.

TIP ► The Tuner button opens a digital guitar tuner that you can use
whenever you have a guitar connected to the computer and the Guitar setting selected in the My Instrument window.

Recording a Part

You are now two clicks away from recording a part. First you'll need to change
the playback to Entire Song, then click the Record button and let the magic
begin.

When you record a part in Magic GarageBand, it's important to set the playhead position first. The recording will always start at the current playhead position.

Also, if you have a section of the song selected, you can record multiple takes of that snippet over and over, then choose the take that you like best. For this part, a single take should do the trick.

1 Change the playback setting to Entire Song, if it isn't set already.

2 Press Return to move the playhead to the beginning of the song.

3 Play the song through once from the beginning and practice playing the Falling Star part wherever you think it sounds good.

If you aren't sure when to play, remember that for a sound like this, less is more. Try playing once during the intro after the other instruments have started. Play a note again at the end of the first verse or at the beginning of the chorus, then another at the ending as the other instruments are playing their final notes.

Too much of this Falling Star sound will make it more of an annoyance than a musical surprise. When in doubt, keep the audience guessing, or wanting more.

4 Click the Record button to start recording.

A red recording region appears above the control bar.

TIP If you play single notes, the name of the note and the octave appear next to the Musical Typing interface. If you play multiple notes, the name of the chord appears instead.

5   Click the Play button to stop recording.

A green Software Instrument region appears above the control bar. The horizontal lines within the region represent the MIDI note events.

If you're really unhappy with your recording and want to do it again, press Cmd-Z to undo, then repeat steps 4 and 5.

NOTE ▶ Guitar, vocals, or other Real Instrument recordings appear as purple regions.

Congratulations! You've recorded an original keyboard part. Next let's open the song in GarageBand to take a look at the finished rock song.

Opening and Saving the Song in GarageBand

Now that your Magic GarageBand song is finished, you'll need to open it in GarageBand to see the finished project, edit the arrangement, add additional tracks, save the project, and, if you like, share it with iTunes.

In this exercise you'll open the finished song in GarageBand and save the finished project.

1   Click the Open in GarageBand button in the lower-right corner of the window.

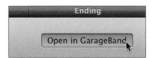

The finished song opens in the GarageBand window.

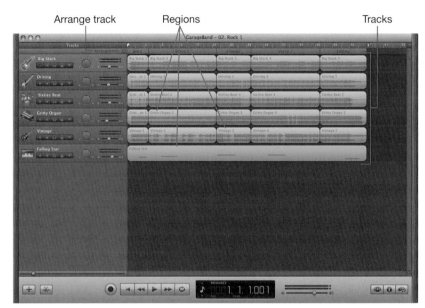

Notice that there's a timeline with a separate track for each instrument part, and that the track names correspond to the Magic GarageBand instruments that you selected earlier.

The arrange track at the top of the window shows each of the different sections of the song (Intro, Verse 1, Chorus, Verse 2, and Ending), and can be edited to rearrange or extend the length of the song.

The short blue regions represent the prerecorded Magic GarageBand parts. The long green region represents the Software Instrument part that you recorded.

Let's save this project as is. Later you can reopen this project and edit, arrange, and mix this song on your own.

For this exercise, you'll do a basic save. To save the project, first you'll open the Save As dialog, and then you'll create a new folder to save all of your GarageBand book projects.

2   Choose File > Save As.

The Save As dialog opens.

3   Type *Magic Rock Song* in the Name field.

NOTE ▶ To expand the Save As dialog, click the downward-pointing arrow at the right side of the Save As field.

4   Click the Desktop icon on the sidebar (left side) of the Save As dialog.

You've now selected the desktop as the location to save your project.

5   Click the New Folder button, located in the lower-left corner of the window.

A New Folder dialog opens.

6   Type *My GarageBand Projects* in the "Name of new folder" field. Click Create.

The new folder is created on your desktop.

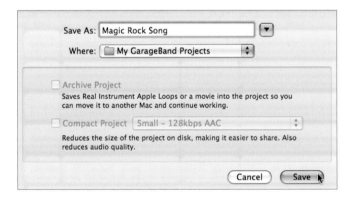

7   In the Save As dialog, click Save.

This saving method is great for finished projects, but takes longer to save, and isn't necessary until you're ready to share the project with other iLife applications.

Your project has been successfully saved to the folder you created on your desktop.

That's it! You've created and saved a rock song. And you have a good working knowledge of the Magic GarageBand Jam interface. In the next lesson you'll learn how to set up and record your own music.

> **NOTE** ▶ The song opened in GarageBand with the name "02. Rock 1." This naming convention is based on the way Magic GarageBand saves your work behind the scenes. *02* and *Rock* represent the genre, and *1* is the version of the Magic GarageBand Rock project you're working on. The next Rock Magic GarageBand Jam session you open and change will be "02. Rock 2" and so on. These Magic GarageBand projects are saved to User > Library > Application Support > GarageBand > Working Copies.

Lesson Review

1. How do you select an instrument in Magic GarageBand Jam?
2. Can you add or change Magic GarageBand instruments?
3. How do you isolate the sound of an instrument in Magic GarageBand?
4. Is there a way to have Magic GarageBand change all of the instruments for you?

Answers

1. You can select an instrument in Magic GarageBand Jam by rolling over the instrument and clicking the instrument.
2. You can change any Magic GarageBand instrument by selecting the instrument and choosing another instrument in the menu. To add an instrument in the My Instrument category, click the Customize button and then choose an instrument from the list.

3. To isolate the sound of an instrument in Magic GarageBand, you can turn on the Solo button in the instrument's mixer.

4. You can have Magic GarageBand automatically change all of the instruments to a different combination by moving to an empty space on the stage, and then clicking the Shuffle Instruments button when it appears.

3

Lesson Files

Time

This lesson takes approximately 60 minutes to complete.

Goals

Choose a project template

Set up an Electric Guitar track

Tune a guitar in the LCD

Use a metronome and a drum track

Work with single-take and multiple-take recordings

Adjust guitar amps and stompboxes

Lesson 3

Recording Music in GarageBand

GarageBand is powerful enough to record and mix a professional-sounding music demo, podcast, or video score, yet simple enough that anyone can use it right out of the box. In fact, you don't have to be a computer science major or audio engineer to record music. You don't even have to be a musician. If you can click a mouse, you can turn your Mac into a basic recording studio—it's really that easy.

This lesson will take you through a Real Instrument recording session in which you'll create a project, select instruments, work with amp effects and stompboxes, adjust input settings, and record tracks for rhythm guitar, bass, and lead guitar.

Recording a Song

This lesson is designed to walk you step by step through a GarageBand recording session. Throughout the next series of exercises you'll follow along with a prerecorded session; you'll also be invited to play along or record your own tracks along the way. No worries if you don't have an instrument connected to the computer. You'll still be able to do everything except tune an instrument and record optional parts.

Choosing a Project Template

GarageBand includes nine project templates. For this recording session we'll use the basic Songwriting template.

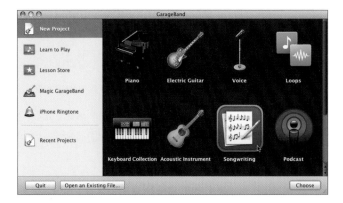

1   Open GarageBand. Choose File > New. In the New Project dialog, click the Songwriting icon, and then click Choose.

2   Name the song *ClassicRockBallad* and save it to the My GarageBand Projects folder on your desktop.

If you didn't complete and save the Magic GarageBand Jam song in Lesson 2, click the New Folder button and create a folder on your Mac's desktop named *My GarageBand Projects*.

NOTE ▸ The bottom portion of the New Project from Template dialog includes controls for setting the tempo, the time signature, and the key of the project before it's created. After it opens, you can also make changes to these project properties in the LCD and in the Track Info pane for the master track.

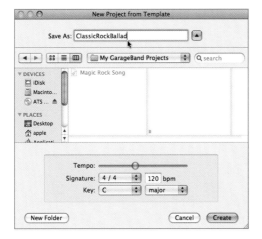

NOTE ▶ You may see the .band file extension showing in the Save As field if the last project that you saved in GarageBand had the file extension showing.

Exploring the GarageBand Window

One of the many advantages of GarageBand is the simplicity of the interface. Like all other iLife applications, GarageBand uses one window as its base of operations. This window is your recording studio.

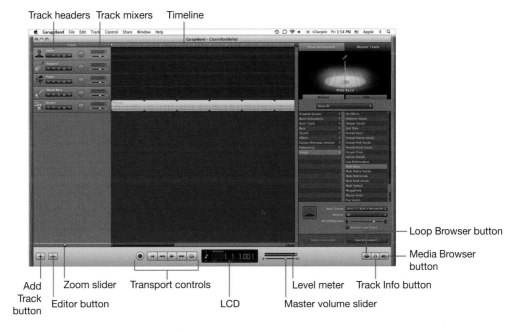

The elements of the GarageBand window and their functions are listed below:

- ▶ Track headers—These show the instrument's icon and name to the left of each track. Each track header includes a Mute button to silence a track, a Solo button to silence all other tracks, a Record Enable button that allows you to record to a specific track, and a Lock Track button to protect the track and its contents from unintended changes. The header also includes a volume slider for adjusting the track volume and a pan dial to adjust the position of the track in the left-to-right stereo field.

- ▶ Timeline—The timeline acts as your music recording and arranging work-space. Consisting of horizontal tracks for each individual instrument, the timeline graphically represents linear time from left to right using a beat ruler at the top of the window. The far-left edge of the timeline represents the beginning of a song.

- ▶ Zoom slider—This slider enables you to zoom in to or out of the timeline.

- ▶ Add Track button—Click this button to add a new track in the timeline.

- ▶ Editor button—This button opens the editor.

- ▶ Transport controls—These controls provide the standard recording and playback buttons to navigate in the timeline. From left to right, they are Record, Go To Beginning, Rewind, Play/Pause, Forward, and Cycle.

- ▶ LCD—Depending on the mode, this display shows the song's properties, the instrument tuner, or the current playhead position in musical time (measures, beats, ticks) or absolute time (hours, minutes, seconds, fractions).

- ▶ Master volume slider—You use this slider to adjust the output volume level of the project.

- ▶ Level meter—This meter indicates the output volume level of a project and includes red warning lights if the level is clipping (too loud).

- ▶ Loop Browser button—This button opens the loop browser.

- ▶ Track Info button—You'll click this button to open the Track Info pane.

- ▶ Media Browser button—Clicking this button opens the Media Browser.

Identifying Regions and Tracks

In the GarageBand window, regions and tracks come in a variety of colors (by type) and sizes, as shown below.

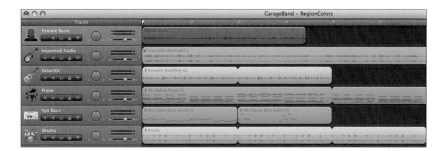

Real Instruments appear as purple, blue, and orange regions. You can record Real Instrument parts in GarageBand through a microphone, guitar, or keyboard that's plugged into the microphone jack on your computer. You can also record Real Instrument parts through other input devices that you connect to your computer. Imported audio files appear as orange regions.

Software Instruments are denoted by green regions and are recorded by means of a USB music keyboard, a MIDI-synthesizer-type keyboard, the GarageBand onscreen keyboard, or Musical Typing (which uses the GarageBand software and your computer's keyboard as the MIDI instrument).

The Songwriting template contains five tracks representing common musical elements used in songwriting. Each track, in turn, can contain individual musical parts, or regions, from a particular instrument. An instrument track may contain only one region, or it may contain many smaller regions—individual takes and retakes, often called overdubs—which, when arranged in a track, are the basic building blocks of an entire instrument's part for a song.

A track can be either a Real Instrument or a Software Instrument track and can be easily identified by the color of the regions within the track or the track header when the track is selected.

1   Click the Voice track header, if it is not already selected, to see the color (type of instrument) assigned to that track.

The blue track header indicates a Real Instrument track.

2   Press Command-I to show the Track Info pane on the right side of the window, if it is not already showing.

> **TIP** ▶ If the Track Info pane is closed, you can double-click a track header to show the Track Info.

3   Click the Piano track header to see an example of a green Software Instrument track.

Notice that the Track Info pane shows a picture of the instrument, indicates the type of instrument (Software Instrument), and highlights the instrument category and specific instrument. You'll work more with Software Instruments in Lesson 4, "Scoring a Movie and Arranging Loops." For now, let's move on with the recording session.

Setting Up an Electric Guitar Track

For this recording session you'll be working with what GarageBand calls Real Instruments. With GarageBand, you can record a real instrument such as a guitar, bass, or keyboard directly into the timeline. You can also use a microphone to record acoustic instruments that don't have an output jack, such as a trumpet, violin, grand piano, drum kit, acoustic guitar, or even vocals.

To record a Real Instrument into the timeline, you have to physically perform or play the part using a real instrument in real time. Let's set up an Electric Guitar track to record the rhythm guitar part.

1   Choose Track > New Track, or click the Add Track button (+) in the lower-left corner of the GarageBand window.

The New Track dialog appears with three track choices: Software Instrument, Real Instrument, and Electric Guitar. The Electric Guitar option is also a Real Instrument track; however, it is specifically designed for the built-in GarageBand amps and stompbox effects.

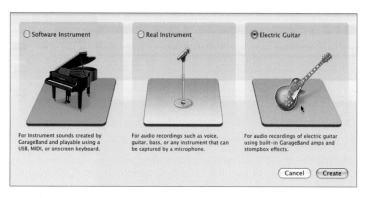

2 In the New Track dialog, select Electric Guitar, then click Create.

A new Real Instrument track named Clean Combo appears in the timeline.

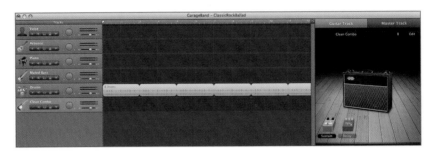

3 Click the amplifier on the right side of the window to see the amplifier controls.

These controls work exactly the same as real amplifier controls, so if you play electric guitar, you should feel right at home.

You can add additional effects before or after recording. In this case you'll keep the recording "clean"—without effects. You'll work with adding effects to change the sound when it's time to lay down the lead guitar part.

Monitoring Your Input

Monitoring is a musical term for listening to yourself play. Just as you would in a recording studio, you'll probably want to monitor your performance when you record a Real Instrument track in GarageBand. If monitoring is turned off, you won't hear the sound of your instrument going to the computer.

Once any instrument part is recorded into the timeline, you'll hear it on playback, just as you would any other region in the timeline.

1   Select the Clean Combo track, if it's not already selected, and make sure that the red Record Enable button is on.

NOTE ▶ If you have an audio interface connected to the computer, you'll be able to record to more than one track at a time. GarageBand allows you to record up to eight Real Instrument tracks and one Software Instrument track simultaneously. Once the instruments are connected to the audio interface, click the Record Enable button on each track that you want to record.

2   Double-click the amplifier to turn it around and to see the input and monitor controls.

3   Change the Monitor pop-up menu to On with Feedback Protection.

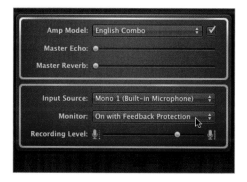

If GarageBand detects feedback, you'll see an alert with the option to change the current setting.

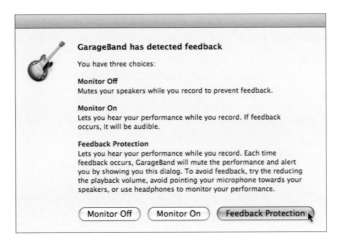

Recording in Stereo vs. Mono

In this exercise, you're working with a single electric guitar with a mono output, so the input into the computer will be mono as well. The Input Source pop-up menu is located above the Monitor pop-up menu in the Track Info pane.

1   Locate the Input Source pop-up menu and choose Mono 1 (Built-in Microphone) if it isn't already selected. This is the default setting.

2   If you have an electric guitar connected to the computer, play a few notes and adjust the Recording Level slider as needed.

Each track in GarageBand has two channels for audio recording and playback: Channel 1 and Channel 2. If you record a track in stereo, you use both channels. If you record mono, you record only Channel 1 or Channel 2.

NOTE ▶ If you don't hear your guitar, check to make sure the volume is turned up on your instrument, and make sure that the input settings on your Mac's Sound preferences are set for the correct input. You'll find more information on setting up your guitar later in this lesson and in the *GarageBand '09 Getting Started* user guide available in the Help menu (Help > GarageBand Help).

Plan Before Recording

There are a few obvious yet essential things to consider before you start recording. First, make sure that the instruments or microphones you intend to use are connected properly and are working. Second, be sure you have enough hard disk space for your recordings. Audio recordings use a fraction of the space of video, but they can accumulate over time, especially if you record many takes. The last thing you want to do is stop your recording session because you're out of disk space.

Stereo audio recorded at CD quality (44.1 kHz) uses around 10 MB of disk space per minute. Ten recorded stereo tracks, for a song that's 3 minutes long, would fill up around 300 MB.

Tuning a Guitar in the LCD

Before you start recording, it's a good idea to tune your guitar. Most professional musicians keep an electronic tuner with them so that they can tune their guitars with precision. GarageBand includes an instrument tuner you can use anytime your instrument is connected to the computer.

If you don't have an instrument handy, just read through the steps so you'll know how to use the tuner the next time you want to record an instrument. William L. Whitacre, who's playing the guitar for this lesson, will be using an electric guitar connected to the computer's audio input jack.

1 In the LCD at the bottom of the window, click the icon at the left and choose the Tuner mode, denoted by a tuning fork.

The time display changes into the instrument tuner.

2 If you have a guitar connected, play an A note.

When you play a note on your instrument, the name of the note appears at the center of the instrument tuner. If your note is perfectly in tune, the display is blue. If it's not, the display is red. The marks on either side of the center show how far off pitch the note is, either left of center if the pitch is flat, or right of center if sharp.

Out of tune   In tune

3 Tune your instrument until the display is blue, indicating that the A string is perfectly tuned.

MORE INFO ▶ You'll find more info on tuning a guitar in the "Tuning" section of the first Learn to Play guitar lesson.

4   Try tuning your instrument for several other notes.

5   When you're finished, click the LCD menu (a tuning fork icon) on the right side of the tuner and choose Project to change the LCD to the default Project mode.

> **NOTE ▶** The instrument tuner can tune any real instrument, even vocals, and it is designed to work with one note at a time. It will not work with chords or combined notes. And sorry, folks, but you can't hook up a bunch of instruments at once and try to tune them all at the same time like an orchestra.

Using a Metronome or Drum Track

The last step before actually recording is to set up either a metronome or a drum track that you can use as a guide to maintain a steady tempo. A metronome is a device used by musicians to keep time. The metronome clicks at a steady beat based on the tempo of the project. You can use GarageBand's built-in metronome both for practicing instrument parts during playback and for recording them.

The built-in metronome automatically plays whenever you record a track, so for those of you who like to use a metronome, you're all set without making any changes to the project.

On the other hand, many musicians prefer to practice and record using a drum track. The Songwriting template includes a prebuilt Drums track for your convenience.

In this exercise you'll explore both methods as you turn the metronome on and off during playback.

Let's begin by listening to the default Drums track in the timeline.

1   Click the Play button in the control bar at the bottom of the window to start playback.

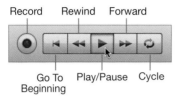

The playhead moves from left to right along the timeline playing the regions that it touches—in this case, a blue Real Instrument Drums region in the Drums track.

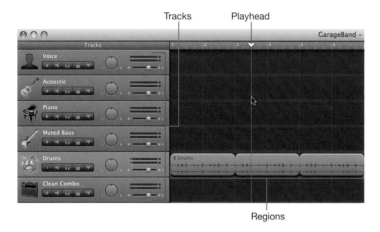

2   Click the Play/Pause button, or press the Spacebar to stop playback, then press Return to move the playhead to the beginning of the timeline.

To hear the metronome during playback, you need to change a setting in General preferences.

3   Choose GarageBand > Preferences, or press Command-, (comma).

The Preferences window opens. If the General pane is not already visible, click the General button.

4   Locate the Metronome options near the top of the General pane.

There are two settings for the metronome: "During recording" and "During playback and recording."

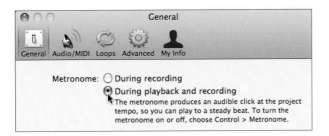

5   Select "During playback and recording," then press Command-W to close
the Preferences window.

6   Start playback to hear the Drums track and metronome at the same time.

7   Click the Mute button on the Drums track to hear the metronome by
itself. Then click the Mute button again to unmute the track.

When a track has been muted, the regions inside the track turn gray.

TIP You can press M to toggle the Mute button on or off for any
selected track. You can also press S to turn the Solo button on or off.
You'll work more with muting and soloing tracks in Lesson 6.

Now that you've listened to both options, let's turn off the metronome and
modify the Drums track.

8   Choose Control > Metronome, or press Command-U to turn off the
Metronome.

Previewing and Adding a Drum Loop

Apple Loops are prerecorded music files that are designed to repeat (loop)
over and over seamlessly as a pattern. Loops are commonly used for drum-
beats, rhythm parts, and other repeating musical sections within a song.

The Drums region in the timeline may be fine for some songs, but the guitar player for this recording session needs something more appropriate for this '50s-style rock ballad. Let's go to the loop browser to find something that will work better for this project.

1   Click the Loop Browser button, or press Command-L to open the loop browser.

2   At the top of the loop browser, click the center button with the musical notes, if the browser isn't already in button view.

Each button represents a type of instrument, genre, or modifier to help you sort through the more than two thousand Apple Loops that come with GarageBand.

NOTE ► Only some of the Apple Loops are installed automatically with iLife '09. If you select a loop that hasn't been installed, you'll see an alert to guide you through downloading and installing the remaining loops. If you see the alert during this exercise, take a few minutes and download the remaining loops. You'll need them for the second project in this lesson.

3   Click the All Drums button. Scroll down the results list until you find the Natural Drum Kit 01 loop, then click that loop to preview it.

Click the loop again to stop the preview. Drag the preview volume slider at the bottom of the loop browser as needed.

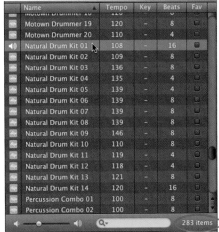

GarageBand includes more than 280 drum loops from which to choose. Feel free to preview some of the other drum loops before moving on to the next step.

The Natural Drum Kit 01 loop will work perfectly with this project. If you're not sure which loop to choose as a drum track for your own project, play your instrument as you preview the loop to find one that feels right for your performance. Remember, you may not end up using this drum track for your finished song—it's just a guide to help you record.

Now that you've selected the Apple Loops file that you'll be using for this session, it's time to delete the old region and add the new one.

4   Move the playhead to the beginning of the timeline.

5   Click the Drums region in the timeline and press Delete.

6   Drag Natural Drum Kit 01 from the results list to the beginning of the Drums track in the timeline.

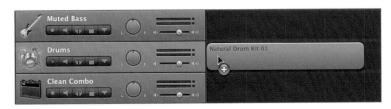

The Natural Drum Kit 01 region appears in the Drums track of the timeline.

7 Close the loop browser.

8 Move the pointer to the upper-right corner of the region until you see the loop pointer (it looks like a curved arrow). Drag the upper-right corner of the region toward the right until it repeats (loops) three times.

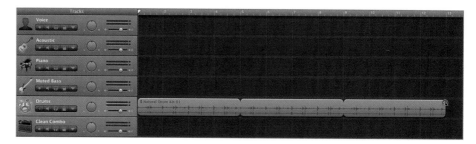

You can identify a loop segment by the rounded notches or indentations at its ends. You don't have to extend a loop for the full length of the original region. If you make the looped section shorter than the original, you'll hear only the notes included in the new loop segment.

Notice that as the loop repeats, you can see notches that show the beginning and end of the original loop within the new region.

9 Play the new Drums track to hear the new drum loop in action. When you're finished, stop playback.

10 If you have a guitar ready to record, practice strumming, play a few chords, or simply riff along with the drum track. You'll be recording that part in a minute.

NOTE ▶ All Apple Loops are designed to match the project key and tempo once they're added to a project. You can see the native key and tempo for a loop in the corresponding column of the results list.

Recording Single Takes

Now that you've completed all of the instrument connections, monitor settings, and input settings and created a drum track, you're finally ready to record.

In this exercise you'll walk through a single-take (rather than multiple-take) recording. A single-take recording begins on a selected track at the playhead position and continues until you stop recording. This is an excellent recording method when you're practicing or just want to record a musical riff, melody, or idea so that you don't forget it. Before you start, it's a good idea to set a count-in so that you'll get four clicks of the metronome before you start the actual recording. In essence, the count-in gives you a "one, two, three, go" so that you don't have to start playing the instant you click Record.

If you don't have a guitar to record, feel free to jump ahead to steps 6 and 7 to save your project, and then open a version with the guitar part already recorded.

1   Choose Control > Count In to turn on the count-in feature.

GarageBand will count in the first 4 beats before recording begins.

2   Select the Clean Combo track to make it active.

TIP▶ The keyboard shortcut to start recording is the R key. This is often easier than using the mouse to click the Record button—especially if you're holding a guitar or another instrument.

3   Press R, or click the Record button, to record your musical riff.

A red region appears in the track as it records.

4   Press the Spacebar to stop recording when you're finished. Play your recording from the beginning to hear how it sounds.

5   Press Command-I to open the Track Info pane, and set the Monitor pop-up menu to Off.

6   Press Command-S to save your project. If you're prompted to save with iLife preview, click No.

     Now let's open a project that has the guitar single-take part already recorded in the timeline.

7   Choose File > Open, and open the file GarageBand09_Book_Files > Lesson_03 > **ClassicRockBallad01**.

     The project opens with a "Clean single take" guitar region on the lowest track of the timeline. Notice that the name of the recorded region is the same as the track header.

8   Play the project from the beginning to listen to the first recorded track in the song.

     NOTE ▶ A new recording will always take on the name of the track in which it is recorded. You can always change the name later. In this case, I changed the name of the track to *Clean single take* before recording so that it would be a more obvious name as an example for this exercise. It's actually the rhythm guitar part and will be named accordingly later.

This performance turned out great, and Bill had obviously practiced it prior to the session. However, he had several variations of the rhythm guitar that he wanted to try. Rather than try each of them as a single-take recording on a different track, the logical alternative would be to do a multiple-take recording.

Recording Multiple Takes

Multiple-take recordings offer several terrific advantages over single-take recordings. For one, you can record a part as many times as you like without stopping. This gives musicians an opportunity to try variations on their performances as well as redo any mistakes or missed notes. Another advantage is that once you're finished, you can choose your favorite take, or split the region and use your favorite take for other sections along the way.

Let's set up another track for a multiple-take recording, then listen to the finished version.

To record multiple takes, you first need to create a cycle region for the entire duration of the part you want to record. Because this piece is only 12 bars (measures) in length, the entire part can be recorded at once. If the song is much longer, it may be better to record shorter sections—such as the intro, verse, and chorus—separately.

1   Click the Cycle button on the control bar to show the yellow cycle region.

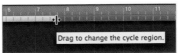

A yellow bar—the cycle region—appears below the beat ruler at the top of the window.

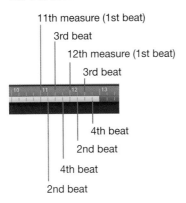

2   Drag the right edge of the cycle region until it extends from the beginning of the song to the 1st beat of the 13th measure.

NOTE ▶ Because the project time signature is 4/4, there are 4 beats per measure. The marks on the ruler represent beats, and the 1st beat of each measure is numbered. Because this song is 12 measures in length, the song ends at the 3rd beat of the 13th measure.

Next you'll need to create a guitar track for the multiple-take recording. Rather than make a new track and adjust all of the settings, you can simply duplicate the existing track.

3   Select the "Clean single take" track, if it isn't already selected. Then choose Track > Duplicate Track, or press Command-D.

A duplicate "Clean single take" track appears below the original. Now all you need to do is change the name of the track and you're ready to record.

4   Click and hold the pointer over the name of the new track in the header until the name field appears. Then type *Clean multi-take* in the name field. When you're finished typing, click anywhere else on the track to close the name field.

That's it—you're ready to record a multiple-take guitar part. If you have a guitar handy and want to try to record along with this song, feel free to continue. If not, you can jump ahead to step 7 to save this version of the project and open the next.

5   Make sure that the "Clean multi-take" track is selected, and click Record or press R. Record three or four full takes of the song.

6   When you're finished, press the Spacebar to stop recording.

The purple multiple-take region includes a yellow number in the upper-left corner. Clicking it brings up the Takes menu, which displays the current take number and allows you to switch between takes.

7 Save your project, then open the **ClassicRockBallad02** project to see a finished multiple-take recording.

The **ClassicRockBallad02** project includes a multiple-take recording in the lowest track of the timeline. The circled number in the upper-left corner of the region shows the current take number in the track. The number of takes that were recorded is added to the name of the region. In this case it says "(4 takes)." There were actually three full takes—the fourth take includes only one note that Bill played after the 12th measure in the third and final take.

NOTE ▶ It's common to record an extra take at the end of a multiple-take recording, because another take usually starts before you can stop recording. You can always disregard that "mis-take" when you select the best performance.

8 Play the song to hear the first take with the other tracks.

This variation of the rhythm guitar sounds pretty good with the original clean single take and the drums. In the next exercise you'll see how to change to the other takes and select the best to use in the track.

Selecting a Best Take

Once you've recorded a multiple-take region, you can use the Takes menu to change to a different take.

1 Click the circled number in the upper-left corner of the "Clean multi-take" region to see the Takes menu.

The Takes menu lists each take, plus an option to delete unused takes or delete the current take.

2   Choose Take 2 from the Takes menu and listen to it with the rest of the song. When you're finished, choose Take 3 and listen to that variation.

Because each take is a different variation of the part, rather than simply a better or worse performance, it's difficult to make a final decision until all of the parts have been recorded.

3   Choose your favorite take from the Takes menu. Then save the project.

Now that you know how to switch to different takes in a multiple-take region, you can feel free to change takes whenever you'd like as you build the rest of the song.

Using Guitar Amps and Stompboxes

The next instrument part for you to lay down (record) for this song is the lead guitar. In this case, the track was already recorded so that you can add effects at this time. In this exercise you'll experiment with GarageBand's guitar amps and stompboxes to modify the sound of the lead guitar track.

These guitar amps and stompboxes were designed to look and respond just like the real hardware, so musicians will immediately feel comfortable in their GarageBand recording studio. In fact, Bill was so blown away by these effects that we had to stop and tweak the lead guitar sound before moving on to record the bass—and he did it himself with no GarageBand experience. In this exercise you'll make the same adjustments to add reverb and delay to the track.

1   Open the project **ClassicRockBallad03**.

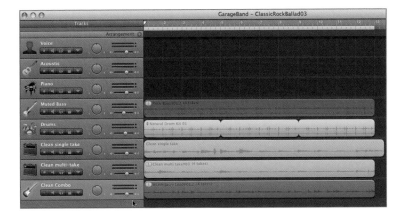

The project opens at the bottom of the timeline with an additional Clean Combo track showing a multiple-take recording. You'll also notice that the Muted Bass track has been muted and that it includes a bass region. Also, the cycle region at the top of the window has been turned on.

2 Play the song—all or part of it—to hear the lead guitar's take 3 with the rest of the tracks. (Keep the Muted Bass track muted for now.)

3 Double-click the Clean Combo track header to show the Track Info pane for that track.

4 Move the pointer to the amplifier icon and hold the pointer there to see a description of that amplifier and its signature sound.

While you hold the pointer over an amplifier, you'll also see two arrow overlays on either side of the amp. You can click the arrows to change amplifiers. The best way to hear the differences in amplifiers is to compare them while the guitar track is playing. The song will automatically repeat for you because the cycle region has been turned on.

5   Play the song and click the arrow on the right or left of the amplifier to change amps during playback.

6   Press S to solo the selected track so that you can hear only the sound of the lead guitar part while you listen to the amplifiers. Press S again to unsolo the track once you've listened to all of the different amplifiers.

7   Click the arrows until you get to the Blackface Combo amplifier. It has a good tone for this type of song. Feel free to choose a different amplifier later.

Let's raise the reverb sound of the amplifier to help the lead guitar stand out a bit more in the song.

8   Click the amplifier to see the controls.

The Reverb knob is in the center of the bottom row.

9   Solo the Guitar track and start playback. Click the center of the Reverb knob, and then drag up to raise the level to around 7 or 8.

> **NOTE** ▶ Dragging up or down on a control knob will raise or lower the level. Because all of the amps have the same controls, any adjustments you make to a control will be retained even if you change to a different amplifier. The amplifier settings will reset, however, if you change instrument sounds using the menu at the top of the Track Info pane.

Great. The reverb is set. Now all that's left is to check the sustain level and turn on the delay. For that, you'll use the stompboxes.

10   Continue playback and click the Sustain stompbox.

A stompbox is so named because it's placed on the floor within reach of the musicians, so that they can quite literally stomp on it to turn it on or off as needed. A light tap of the toe also works, but that is much less dramatic onstage. In this example, the Sustain stompbox looks exactly like the real thing (dent included).

The button to stomp on or off is located near the bottom, where it's easy to reach with a foot in the real world or with a pointer in GarageBand. If a stompbox is turned off, the name will be dimmed on the stage, much like the Delay stompbox in this project.

NOTE ▶ The default setting for sustain is on for all of the guitar amplifiers. That's a good thing, because in almost every musical scenario, instruments and even vocals sound better with a little sustain or reverb.

11 Click the On/Off switch for the Squash Compressor (sustain) stompbox to
hear the difference in the track with and without sustain.

The red LED lights up when the stompbox is on. When you're finished,
make sure that it's on.

12 Click the Delay stompbox and turn it on. Then drag the Mix knob upward
to about 35%. When you're finished, unsolo the track to hear the modified
guitar sound in the track.

13 Double-click either stompbox on the stage below the amplifier to see all
12 stompboxes.

14 You can add stompboxes by dragging them up to the yellow rectangles below the amplifier. To remove a stompbox, simply drag it from the stage.

Now that you've seen how to change amplifiers and stompboxes, let's look at adjusting their settings.

Saving Effects Settings

Once you've adjusted the amplifier and stompbox effects to your liking, you can save those settings so that you'll be able to use them again on another project.

1   Click the Save Setting button at the bottom of the Track Info pane.

2   Type *W L Whitacre Lead* in the "Save as" field. Then click Save.

> **TIP** ▶ You can save as many effects settings as you'd like. You can also delete any of your custom settings if you no longer need them by clicking the Delete Setting button.

3   Click the pop-up menu at the top at the Track Info pane to see a list of all of the available Electric Guitar sounds. GarageBand includes 38 guitar effects presets.

4   Choose a sound from the list and listen to it during playback.

   The amplifier and stompboxes change automatically to match the preset.

5   Choose W L Whitacre Lead from the My Settings area at the bottom of the presets menu to change back to the customized settings for this track.

Working with an Acoustic Guitar Track

The last guitar part for you to lay down is the acoustic guitar. Recording an acoustic guitar is almost the same as recording an electric guitar within the GarageBand interface. The difference is that acoustic guitars don't use amplifiers or stompboxes for effects, and the controls for input and monitoring appear at the bottom of the Track Info pane.

Because the Songwriting template includes an acoustic track for the guitar, you don't need to create a new track. Otherwise, you could just create a new track and choose Real Instrument as the type of track.

Let's set up the acoustic track to record a part.

1   Double-click the Acoustic track header to show the track in the Track Info pane.

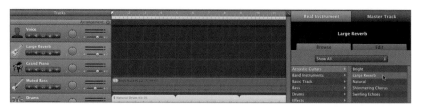

2   Select Large Reverb from the Acoustic Guitars effects list.

The track header updates to match the name of the effects preset applied to that track. Rather than record an entirely new region with an acoustic guitar, let's duplicate the "Clean single take" region and place it in the acoustic track. Doubling a version of the same part is a great way to *fatten* the sound of the part.

3   Option-drag the "Clean single take" region and drop the duplicate at the beginning of the Large Reverb track.

To Option-drag you simply select a region and hold down the Option key while dragging; this creates a duplicate region.

4   Listen to the song with the doubled guitar regions. Then press Command-S to save your progress.

Voilà! You created an acoustic guitar part without recording a new one. You can also do the same thing in reverse and drag an acoustic guitar part into an Electric Guitar track to double the tracks to sound like two different types of guitars playing the same part.

> **NOTE** ▸ The input source, monitoring, and recording level controls for an acoustic guitar (Real Instrument) track are located at the bottom of the Track Info pane. You'll find more info on these settings at the beginning of this lesson.

Editing Multiple-Take Regions

You already know how to select takes within a multiple-take recording. In this exercise you'll split a multiple-take region into three separate regions so that you can use a different take for each part. For this example you'll work with the Muted Bass track. First, you'll unmute the track, and then select a different bass effects preset to enhance the sound.

If you haven't completed all of the steps prior to this exercise, open the project **ClassicRockBallad04** to catch up.

1   Click the blue Mute button on the Muted Bass track to unmute the track. Play the project to hear the bass part.

   The bass part is a bit too subtle for this song, so let's find a better bass sound for the track.

2   Double-click the Muted Bass track header to show the track in the Track Info pane, if it isn't already showing.

3   Start playback. Select Bass from the instrument category list on the left, then click various bass sounds from the instrument list in the right column to hear them with the song. When you're finished trying different sounds, choose Colorful Bass from the list.

The track name updates to reflect the new track instrument sound.

4   Press Command-I to hide the Track Info pane.

   TIP ▶ Before trying to split a track, it's a good idea to zoom in so that you can move the playhead more precisely along the timeline. The more you zoom in, the finer increments of movement you can achieve using the Left Arrow and Right Arrow keys.

5   Drag the timeline's zoom slider to around the middle of the slider control to zoom in on the timeline.

The LCD is currently in the Measures mode. Your goal is to move the playhead to the 4th beat of the 7th measure (7.4.1.001 on the LCD).

6   Press the Right Arrow key until the LCD shows 7.4.1.001.

7   Select the Rock Bass region in the Colorful Bass track if it's not already selected.

8   Press Command-T, or choose Edit > Split to split the selected track at the playhead position.

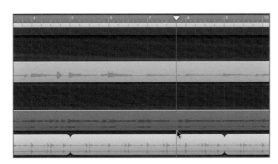

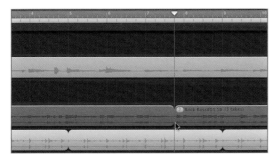

The track now contains two regions.

9   If necessary, change the second region in the Colorful Bass track to take 2. Leave the first bass region set to take 3. Listen to the edited track with the rest of the song.

10   When you're finished, press Command-S to save the finished song. Press Command-W to close the project window. If you're prompted to save with iLife preview, click No.

> NOTE ▶ To hear the finished song, including a voice track from William L. Whitacre commenting on the song, open the project **ClassicRockBallad05**.

There you have it. Now you can split your multiple-take regions so that you can use your favorite combination of performances within the same track. You've also reached the end of the recording session. In Lesson 6, "Mixing Music and Effects," you'll learn how to arrange sections of a song, mix track volume levels, and add effects to improve the overall sound.

Lesson Review

1.   Where is the tuner located in GarageBand?

2.   What are the two most common ways to keep musical time as you record a part in GarageBand?

3.   When can you change the sound of a guitar track?

4.   What types of effects are unique to Electric Guitar tracks in GarageBand?

5.   Where do you change the instrument for a track?

Answers

1.   The tuner is one of the modes in the LCD, which is located at the bottom of the GarageBand window.

2.   Turn on the metronome or use a drum track to help you keep musical time as you record.

3.   You can change a guitar track's sound either before or after recording.

4.   GarageBand includes amps and stompbox effects that can be used with Electric Guitar tracks.

5.   You can change a track's instrument in the Track Info pane.

4

Lesson Files
GarageBand09_Book_Files > Lesson_04 > TouchPetsMOCKUP.mov

GarageBand09_Book_Files > Lesson_04 > TouchPetsScore00 – 05d

GarageBand09_Book_Files > Lesson_04 > TouchPetsTrailer.mov

Time
This lesson takes approximately 90 minutes to complete.

Goals
Import a movie from the Media Browser

Edit and arrange loops

Work with Software Instrument parts

Change track instruments

Transpose in the editor

Copy and paste in the timeline

Add sound effects to a project

Archive the finished project

Scoring a Movie and Arranging Loops

How you score a movie depends greatly on the scope of the project. Feature film scores often require composers, large recording stages, and full orchestras. Smaller projects, such as training videos, corporate projects, or home movies, can easily be scored using GarageBand.

Not only can you create your own music for your iLife projects and QuickTime–compatible video files, but you can also choose from hundreds of finished music pieces and sound effects to complete the soundtrack.

In this lesson, you'll use Apple Loops to create an original score for an iPhone or iPod touch game trailer. Though you'll be creating music for a video, the composing and arranging techniques you'll learn can be used to build your own original music.

First you'll import a finished video. Then you'll create a soundtrack from scratch using some of the Apple Loops and sound effects that come with GarageBand. Along the way, you'll also learn some music arranging techniques for moving musical parts, doubling tracks, changing track instruments, and even transposing, or changing the pitch of, a region. You'll also learn how to place sound effects at your fingertips as you design your own Musical Typing instrument track and save the customized settings.

Scoring a QuickTime Movie

To score an iMovie project, you can access the project through the Media Browser as long as it was saved with iLife preview. In this case you'll be working with a finished QuickTime movie rather than an iMovie project, so the first step is to add the file to the Media Browser. The easiest way to do that is to copy the movie file to the Movies folder on your Mac.

1   Open the Finder window on your computer.

2   Locate **TouchPetsMOCKUP.mov** in the Lesson_04 folder on your desktop. The full path is GarageBand09_Book_Files > Lesson_04 > **TouchPetsMOCKUP.mov**.

3   Drag **TouchPetsMOCKUP.mov** to the Movies icon in the Finder sidebar.

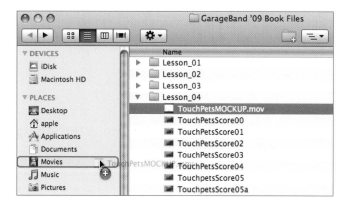

Now that the movie is in the Movies folder, you're ready to create a project and build the score in GarageBand.

Creating a Movie Score Project

GarageBand includes a Movie template: an empty project with a movie track already showing. Let's create a movie project using the template, and then add the video clip to the movie track.

1   Open GarageBand if it isn't already open, and choose File > New. Double-click the Movie icon in the New Projects template list to create a movie project.

2   Name the project *TouchPetsScore*, and save it to the My GarageBand
        Projects folder on your desktop. If you didn't create a folder in the earlier
        exercise, go ahead and create one now.

3   Click Create to open the new **TouchPetsScore** project.

Movie track   Media Browser

Editor

The **TouchPetsScore** project opens with the movie track, editor, and Media
Browser showing.

Previewing a Movie in the Browser

The Media Browser contains buttons for various types of media files (audio,
photos, movies). This provides an easy way to navigate to the media files you
want to use.

The Movies pane of the Media Browser may include iTunes if you've created
your own MP4 files compressed for your video iPod or have downloaded video
podcasts. (Some tracks that are purchased from the iTunes store are "protected"
media. These songs will not appear in the Media Browser.) You can add other
folders to the Media Browser by dragging them there, so you can access media
files anywhere on your computer from within GarageBand.

Before you import the video file to your project, it's a good idea to preview it.
Finding the right video file in this case is easy because you already know which

movie you'll be using. However, in your real-life workflow you may have dozens, or even hundreds, of video clips in your Media Browser, and the selection process may not be as easy.

There are two simple ways to preview a video clip in the Media Browser: Select the file and click the Play button, or double-click the clip.

1   In the Media Browser, double-click the **TouchPetsMOCKUP.mov** clip. It's the white icon with the ngmoco:) logo.

The movie icon becomes a small preview of the movie. What you're watching is a trailer (sans music) for the TouchPets Dogs game by ngmoco:). This game is designed exclusively for iPhone and iPod touch, and it needs a score that captures the fun, energy, and personality of the virtual puppies. This type of project is a composer's dream, not only because it sparks the imagination to infinite musical opportunities, but also because it can be scored with nearly any genre of music. Feel free to try your own score after this lesson.

2   Press the Spacebar to stop the preview.

Importing a Video File from the Media Browser

You can import any iMovie project or QuickTime–compatible video file from the Media Browser. The movie you'll use in this lesson was created in Apple's

Final Cut Pro and saved as a QuickTime movie. Let's add the movie to our
GarageBand project.

1   Drag **TouchPetsMOCKUP.mov** to the movie track.

GarageBand generates thumbnails for the track to represent the video
clips. It also adds a track called Movie Sound and creates a new AIFF file
that contains the soundtrack of the movie. The original movie file remains
unchanged.

NOTE ▶ The video file always starts at the beginning of the project. Once
added to a project, video files can't be edited or repositioned in the timeline. The Movie Sound track is a Real Instrument track, and it includes an
orange (imported) Real Instrument region.

2   Click the Media Browser button in the bottom corner of the window, or
press Command-R to hide the Media Browser.

3   Click the movie track to show the editor.

NOTE ▶ A project can contain only one movie file. If you import a movie
file into a project that already contains one, you'll see a dialog asking if
you want to replace the existing movie with the new one.

Your project is now ready to score.

4   Choose File > Save, or press Command-S to save your work so far.

Watching the Movie in the Timeline

GarageBand includes a floating Movie Preview window that you can resize and place anywhere on your screen. The Movie Preview window is available for viewing your video as long as the movie track is showing. Because this project is based on video instead of music, you can change the LCD mode to Time (timecode) rather than Measures.

1   In the LCD, choose Time from the LCD menu. The playhead's position in absolute time appears (hours:minutes:seconds.fractions).

2   Press the End key to move the playhead to the end of the project.

The LCD indicates that the project is about 1 minute and 4 seconds in length.

3   Click the Preview button on the movie track header to show the Movie Preview window.

4   Play the project from the beginning to see the movie file in the Movie Preview window. This time, as you watch, try to identify the three main sections of the TouchPets trailer.

> **TIP** ▶ Drag the lower-right corner of the Movie Preview window to resize it. Drag the top of the window to move it to a different location on the screen.

Creating a Cycle Region for Scoring

You probably noticed that the three main sections of the trailer include a beginning montage of puppies, solo shots of the TouchPets breeds and profiles, and an information section at the end. The secret to scoring a project like this is to identify each section and modify the music to fit it. In this exercise you'll create a cycle region for the first section to make it easier to audition and select appropriate loops.

1   Press Command-E to hide the editor. Make sure the playhead is at the beginning of the project by pressing the Return key.

2   Press C to show the cycle region.

3   Drag the zoom slider toward the right (about two-thirds of the way) until you see each second listed in the beat ruler at the top of the window.

> **TIP** ▶ You can use the LCD to navigate to a specific time by double-clicking the numbers in the display and typing the desired time. Press the Right Arrow or Left Arrow key to select a different field within the LCD. Press Return to send the playhead to the location in the display. You can also move the playhead in the timeline by pressing the Left Arrow and Right Arrow keys.

4 Create a cycle region between 6 seconds (6.000) and 19 seconds (19.000).

5 Play the cycle region to see the first section that you'll be scoring.

Working with Loops

Now that you've viewed the project and identified its three main sections, it's time to add music. In the next series of exercises, you'll create a basic percussion and bass piece in the timeline, using some of the professional-quality pre-recorded Apple Loops that come with GarageBand.

You'll use Apple Loops as the primary building block for your score. Apple Loops are prerecorded music files that can be used to add drum beats, rhythmic elements, and other repeating patterns to a project. Loops contain musical patterns that can be repeated seamlessly as well as combined into new musical arrangements. You can extend a loop to fill any amount of time in a project.

There are two primary strategies for scoring video (or composing music in general). You can choose a melody that fits the mood or tells a musical story, and then add rhythm or percussion, or both, to fill out the song. Or you can start with percussion or rhythm tracks to capture the tempo or action of a piece and then, if you wish, add a melody to finish off the score.

> **NOTE** ▶ There are two types of Apple Loops: Real Instrument loops and Software Instrument loops. The color of a loop's icon indicates which type each loop is. Real Instrument loops (which are recordings of real instruments) have a blue icon with an audio waveform. Software Instrument loops (which are generated by the computer using a synthesizer) have a green icon with a musical note.

Browsing and Adding Loops to the Project

For this project, you'll create an original percussion-based piece of music using Apple Loops that come with GarageBand. This process involves a fair amount of experimentation as you search for combinations to use. For the purpose of this lesson, the choices will be identified for you. Your goal in this exercise is to create a piece of music that works well with the video.

To start, let's create a cycle region around the intro montage (from around 6 seconds to 19 seconds) to make it easier to find a percussion loop that works with that section of the trailer.

> **NOTE ▶** Though it's common to use markers to set scoring cues in a video project, they aren't always necessary. Because you'll be working with markers in Lesson 7 to create a podcast, we'll focus on other techniques during this lesson.

1   Play the cycle region to see the gait of the walking dogs. Your goal is to find something with the same energy and fun as the virtual pups.

2   Press Command-L to open the loop browser. Click the center button (with the musical notes) to open the button view if the loop browser isn't already in that view, and then click the All Drums button.

3   Press the Spacebar to start playback, then click one of the drum loops in the list to audition it with the video. Try auditioning several different loops.

Funny how so many seem to perfectly fit the little doggies' footfalls. They must have been programmed in perfect musical time.

4   Scroll down to Motown Drummer 06 in the list and audition the loop with the video.

This loop will work perfectly for the intro.

5   Pause playback, then drag the Motown Drummer 06 loop from the results list in the loop browser to the empty space below the Movie Sound track. Place the beginning of the loop so that it starts at the beginning of the cycle region (00:06 on the beat ruler).

TIP ▶ To place the loop at the desired position, use the alignment guide (a vertical dark line) that appears when you add the loop to the timeline.

The loop is added to the timeline and lasts for 4 seconds—it needs to be extended to the end of the cycle region. First, let's change the zoom level of the timeline so that you can see the entire cycle region.

6   Drag the zoom slider toward the left until you see the entire cycle region (near the halfway mark on the slider control).

7   Drag the upper-right corner of the Motown Drummer 06 loop until it extends four full times. Don't worry if the fourth loop extends beyond the cycle region. You'll fix that shortly.

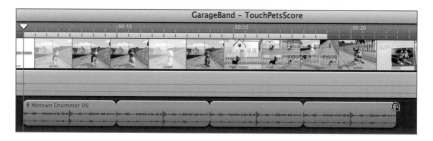

8   Play the project to see and hear the results. Pay close attention to the way the drums match the pup montage.

The beat is close, but it just doesn't feel quite right yet. The drums will work better if they start a bit later. Also, the project needs an additional drum loop or a change when four pups appear onscreen at the same time.

Using Alignment Guides and Snapping

Adding, resizing, and arranging regions in the timeline often require very precise movements. GarageBand includes alignment guides and snapping to help you work with more precision and accuracy.

When you work with musical elements, it's a good idea to change the timeline to musical time so the loops stay in time with each other.

1   Change the LCD to Measures mode.

2   Choose Control > Show Alignment Guides to turn on the guides. Also make sure that Snap to Grid is selected.

3   Drag the drum loop right in the timeline to the first tick mark (between the 1st and 2nd beat of the 4th measure). Use the yellow alignment guide below the cycle region to help you see the new position of the region.

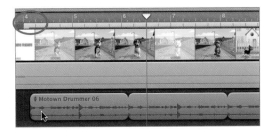

4   Play the loop in the new position to see how well the slight change fits with the white flashes and the doggy trots.

NOTE ▶ Normally, songs are built entirely in musical time, with loops and recordings starting on even measures or even beats. Because the percussion in this piece is used not only to provide music but also to accent movement and action, the arrangement will be motivated by the video timing rather than purely musical timing.

Trimming a Loop

Sometimes you'll find that an Apple Loops file is too long for your purposes, or that you want to use only a portion of a loop in your project. Dragging the upper-right side of a loop with the loop pointer extends or shortens the length of time that the loop plays or repeats.

You can also shorten the loop itself. To shorten a loop, drag either the lower-left or the lower-right side of the loop with the resize pointer. If you shorten the loop from its beginning (left edge), you're trimming the actual content of the loop. Once you've trimmed the beginning of a loop, any loop segments you create by extending the right edge will reflect the new shortened loop, rather than the original.

In this scoring project, the drum loop works great for the intro but starts to feel repetitive as the section progresses. Also, the drum sound should change when the shot changes to a split screen with four pups at once. Let's shorten the loop already in the timeline, then add two more loops and trim as needed.

1   Drag the upper-right corner of the loop toward the left and shorten it to the tick mark between the first 2 beats of the 9th measure (9.1.3.001).

2   Press Command-L to open the loop browser, if it isn't already open, then click the All Drums button and find the Motown Drummer 07 loop in the results list.

3   Drag Motown Drummer 07 to the timeline below the first drum track, and place it between the 1st and 2nd beats of the 8th measure (8.1.3.001).

4   From the loop browser, drag Motown Drummer 08 to the timeline below the second drum track, and place it so that it ends at the 3rd beat of the 10th measure (10.3.1.001).

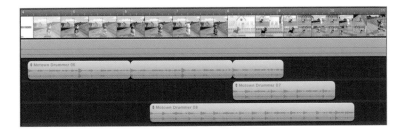

TIP ▶ When making precision movements of regions in the timeline, use the playhead and the LCD to find a specific position, then align the loop to the playhead.

5 Click the Reset button located at the upper left of the loop browser. Play the project to hear how the loops work together in the timeline.

6 Move the playhead to 9.3.1.001. Trim the beginning of the Motown Drummer 08 loop to the playhead position. Play the project again to hear the difference.

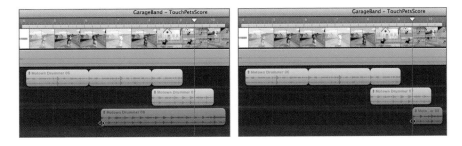

7 Press C to hide the cycle region, and Command-S to save your progress.

Wow. What a difference two additional loops and a quick trim can make! In a few seconds you've accomplished several feats of musical magic. The drum beat picks up just as multiple dogs appear, so it feels like their combined sound, and the fun drum hit at the end of the third loop perfectly matches the running and jumping movements of the little white Westie as well as the dachshund's slide. Nice work! If your project doesn't sound right, or you missed a step, open the project **TouchPetsScore00** in the Lesson_04 folder to catch up.

Project Tasks

If you completed the last few exercises, you have all the skills you need to add and arrange the drum loops for the next section of the project. Each bullet point shows you the name of the loop in the loop browser's results list, which track to place it on, and where to position it. Have fun. If you'd like to skip this practice and jump ahead, feel free to open the project **TouchPetsScore01** in the Lesson_04 folder.

> **NOTE ▸** You'll need to release the loop into the track before you can align it with precision. The alignment guides appear dark gray instead of yellow if the cycle region is hidden.

- ▸ Hold the pointer over the name of each of the Kits tracks and add a number to the track name, so that from top to bottom they read *Kits 01, Kits 02, Kits 03.*

- ▸ Click the Bongo button in loop browser. Drag Bongo Grove 04 to the Kits 02 track, starting at 10.2.1.001. Click the Reset button when finished.

- ▸ Click the All Drums button in loop browser. Drag Club Dance Beat 001 to the Kits 01 track, starting at 10.3.3; trim the right side to end at 12.2.1.

- ▸ Drag Club Dance Beat 002 to the Kits 03 track, starting at 11.3.3; trim the right side to end at 12.4.1.

- ▸ Drag Classic Rock Beat 05 to Kits 02 track, starting at 12.3.1; trim the right side to end at 14.3.3.

- ▸ Drag Lounge Jazz Drums 01 to the Kits 01 track, starting at 14.2.1; trim the right side to end at 16.4.3.

▶ Drag Hip Hop Beat 03 to the Kits 02 track, starting at 16.3.3; trim the right side to end at 19.3.3.

▶ Drag Ambient Beat 01 to the Kits 01 track, starting at 19.1.1; trim the right side to end at 21.1.1.

Your finished project should look like the screen below. Be sure to save your progress when you're finished.

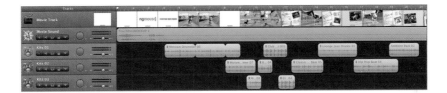

Working with Software Instrument Loops

Up until now you've been using Real Instrument loops in this lesson. In the next series of exercises you'll work with Software Instrument loops to create the bass tracks for this score.

If you didn't complete all of the steps in the earlier exercises, open the project **TouchPetsScore01** to catch up.

1   In the loop browser, click the Reset button to remove the keyword filters.

2   Click the Bass button, then select Woody Latin Bass 05 in the results list.

3   Drag Woody Latin Bass 05 to the empty space below the Kits 03 track and move the loop in the timeline so that it starts at 10.3.3.

4   Press Command-L to hide the loop browser.

Notice that the region is green and that the notes look like dashes instead of an audio waveform. That's because Software Instruments record completely flexible note *events*, rather than recorded sound.

5   Move the playhead to 21.2.3, then drag the upper-right corner of the loop toward the right so that it ends at the playhead position.

6 Play the project to hear how the bass works with percussion loops.

Not bad, but not great either. You probably hear the potential, but also notice that too much of anything starts to sound repetitive and boring.

TIP When you add a Software Instrument loop, you can convert it to a Real Instrument loop. Real Instrument loops require less processing power for playback. This allows you to use more tracks and effects in a project without affecting your computer's performance. To change a Software Instrument loop to a Real Instrument loop, drag it to a Real Instrument track, or choose GarageBand > Preferences and in the Loops pane, select the Convert to Real Instruments checkbox.

Splitting a Loop Region

Given that the percussion changes for each dog personality, it would be nice to have the bass part change as well.

By splitting a loop, you'll create parts that can be modified individually. This makes it easier to use loops from the same family when you're building a song. In this exercise you'll split the bass loop into smaller sections, then change them into musical variations.

1 Select the green bass region in the Acoustic Bass track to select it, if it isn't already selected.

2 Move your playhead to 12.3.1 and press Command-T, or Choose Edit > Split. (This position matches the beginning of the Classic Rock Beat region in the Kits 02 track.)

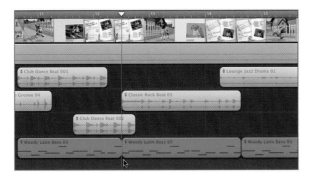

The region automatically splits again at 14.3.1 to ensure that the new segment will loop properly. This is a good thing and saves you from splitting the loop there manually.

3   Split the bass region again at 16.3.3 and 19.1.1.

4   Press Command-S to save your progress.

> **NOTE ▶** To make it easier to work with loops, they're often grouped into families. You'll see loops in the loop browser that have the same name, but with different numbers at the end. For example, Woody Latin Bass 04 and Woody Latin Bass 05 belong to the same family. Loops in the same family often work well together musically.

5   Click an empty area of the timeline to deselect any loops.

6   In the timeline, select the second instance of the loop Woody Latin Bass 05.

7   Click the up and down arrows in the upper-left corner of the loop region to see a menu of other loops in the same family. Choose Woody Latin Bass 08 from the menu.

8 Set the third bass region to Woody Latin Bass 03, and the last bass region to Woody Latin Bass 08.

9 Play the project to hear the different bass parts, and then save your progress.

Using Advanced Arranging Techniques

Now that you have built the basic percussion and bass tracks, it's time to use more advanced techniques for finishing the tracks. In the next few exercises you'll create new tracks to double regions, change a Software Instrument loop's instrument, and even transpose a loop to make a doubled part sound more interesting. Finally, you'll copy and paste loops within the timeline to finish the score.

If you didn't finish the earlier exercises, open the project **TouchPetsScore02** to catch up.

Changing Track Instruments

One of the most exciting things about Software Instrument parts is that they will change to any Software Instrument that you assign to the track. In the previous lesson, you doubled guitar parts to enhance a song. In this case you'll double the bass parts but change the instrument of the doubled part to make it more interesting. For this exercise you'll make three new Software Instrument tracks from the original Acoustic Bass track.

1 Select the Acoustic Bass track header and press Command-D three times.

You should now have four Acoustic Bass tracks in the timeline. The top two bass tracks will keep their original instruments. Let's change the instruments for the lower two bass tracks.

2   Double-click the third Acoustic Bass track header to show the Track Info pane for that track.

3   On the Track Info pane, select Bass as the instrument category (left column) and Sub Synth Bass as the specific instrument (right column).

A dialog appears to warn you that you're changing the track instrument.

4   Click Continue. Notice that the track header changes to Sub Synth Bass.

5   Select the fourth Acoustic Bass header and change the track instrument to Trance Bass, also in the Bass instrument category.

6   Press Command-I to hide the Track Info pane.

Duplicating Regions in the Timeline

Now that you've created the different bass tracks, you can duplicate some of the bass regions and place the copies in the different tracks. In the previous lesson you learned how to Option-drag to duplicate a guitar region. You'll use that same technique here to double the bass parts. All the regions that you duplicate will start on the original Acoustic Bass track.

1   Select the second bass region in the timeline, then press and hold the Option key while dragging the region down to the Sub Synth Bass track.

Notice the handy vertical yellow alignment guides to help you keep the duplicate aligned with the original.

2   Option-drag the third bass region and place the duplicate on the second Acoustic Bass track.

3   Option-drag the fourth bass region and place the duplicate on the Sub Synth Bass track.

4   Option-drag the last bass region and place the duplicate on the Trance Bass track.

5   Save your project, then play it to hear the modified bass parts.

As you can hear, the bass parts are more interesting and seem to work well with the different puppy personalities. If you didn't complete all the previous steps, open **TouchPetsScore02a** to catch up.

Transposing a Region in the Editor

The editor is a separate pane below the timeline that you can use to edit a region or to modify the region's pitch or timing. In this exercise you'll look at a Software Instrument region in the editor, then change that region's pitch so that it plays one octave higher. You'll work more with the editor in Lesson 5.

1   Press Command-E to open the editor.

2   Select the bass region in the second Acoustic Bass track to show it in the editor.

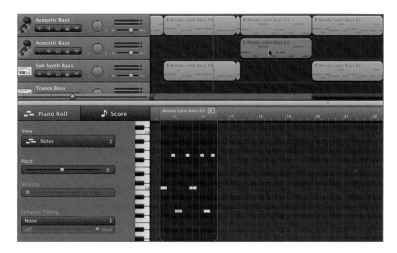

The Software Instrument region appears in the piano roll view (dashes) in the editor.

3   Click Score to change to the score view in the editor.

NOTE ▶ An octave has 12 semitones, including sharps and flats. To play the same note one octave higher, you simply change the pitch to 12. To make it one octave lower, you change the pitch to –12. Changing the pitch of a musical part is called *transposing*. For Software Instrument regions, you can also drag individual notes, or groups of notes to different positions in the Score view in the editor to change their pitch accordingly.

4   In the editor, drag the Pitch slider to the right until it reads 12.

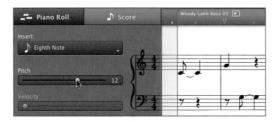

The musical notation adjusts accordingly, and a small *+12* appears in the lower-left corner of the region that you transposed in the timeline.

5   Press Command-E to hide the editor. Then play the transposed bass section in the timeline to hear how it sounds. The higher pitch for the bass seems a little peppier and happier, which fits perfectly with the personality of the Labrador pup.

6   Save your progress.

Copying and Pasting in the Timeline

The last advanced arranging technique that you'll learn in this lesson is how to copy and paste sections that you've already created so that you don't have to duplicate your work. In this exercise you'll copy a group of percussion and bass loops and paste them at the end of the timeline to build the final part of the score.

To select a group of clips in the timeline, Command-click the clips. If they're together, you can click near one and drag to select them all.

If you didn't complete all the steps in the previous section, open the project **TouchPetsScore03** to catch up.

1   Move the pointer to the front of the timeline until you see the first group of drum loops.

2   Click the empty space just before the first drum loop on the Kits 01 track, then drag down and to the right until you select all three of the Motown Drummer regions.

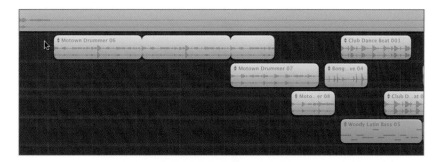

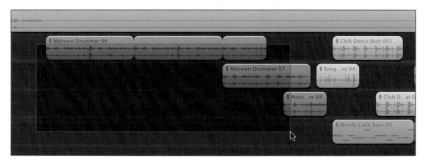

3   Choose Edit > Copy, or press Command-C to copy the selected clips.

4   Move the playhead to 21.1.1 in the timeline and choose Edit > Paste, or press Command-V.

The drum regions appear on the same tracks as they were copied from, but they start at the beginning of the 21st measure.

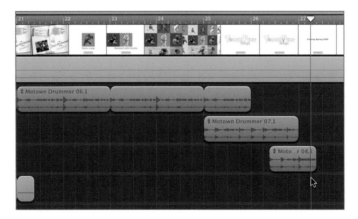

5   Select both of the Woody Latin Bass 08 regions in the timeline between the 19th and 21st measures. Copy the selected regions and paste them so that they start at the beginning of the 25th measure.

6   Select and copy the two Woody Latin Bass 05 regions in the timeline and paste them so that they start at the beginning of the 27th measure. You'll paste over part of the Woody Latin Bass 08 region intentionally.

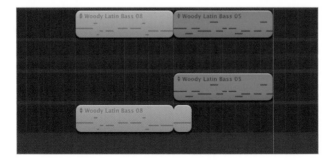

7   Save your progress.

NOTE ▶ If you didn't complete all the steps, feel free to open the project **TouchPetsScore03a** to catch up.

Project Tasks

This basic score is nearly complete. All that's left is adding a few additional loops and cleaning up some loose ends. You have the skills, so now is a good time to put them to work. If you would rather skip this practice, feel free to open the project **TouchPetsScore04**.

▶ Shorten the Motown Drummer 06 loop at the end of the Kits 01 track so that it ends at the beginning of the 24th measure (24.1.1).

▶ Move the Motown Drummer 08 loop at the end of the Kits 03 track so that it begins at the 24th measure (24.1.1).

▶ Move the Motown Drummer 07 loop on the Kits 02 track so that it starts at the beginning of the 22nd measure. Extend the upper-right corner so that it ends at 24.2.1.

▶ In the loop browser, find the Hip Hop Beat 02 loop and add it to the Kits 01 track so that it starts at the beginning of the 25th measure (25.1.1) and ends at the beginning of the 28th measure (28.1.1).

▶ In the loop browser, find the Hip Hop Beat 03 loop and add it to the Kits 02 track so that it starts at the beginning of the 27th measure (27.1.1) and ends at the beginning of the 30th measure (30.1.1).

▶ Shorten the Woody Latin Bass 08 region in the Trance Bass track so that it ends at the beginning of the 27th measure. Move the loop up to the Sub Synth Bass track.

▶ Split the Woody Latin Bass 05 loop in the Sub Synth Bass track at 28.1.1 and move the second half after the split down to the Trance Bass track.

▶ Shorten the two Woody Latin Bass 08 loops used with the Jack Russell pup so that they both end at 14.3.1.

When you finish, don't forget to watch the project and save your progress.

Great work! Sure, the tracks could use some mixing (adjustments to the levels), which you'll learn in Lesson 6, but the foundation is there, and that was the goal for this lesson. To see this version with all of the changes applied, open the project **TouchPetsScore04**.

Working with Sound Effects

Now that the music is in place, it's time to have some fun adding sound effects to the project. You've probably seen an animal bloopers TV show that includes funny music and sound effects when animals slip, fall, bump into things, or act wacky. It's mostly the footage that makes these shows funny, but the sound effects add a little extra humor that might push a chuckle into a full-blown laugh. This is your opportunity to add sound effects to the animated TouchPets footage. Keep in mind that GarageBand includes lots of "serious" sounds, too. In fact, a well-placed siren will work very nicely to accent the Labrador pup's heroic personality.

There are two primary ways to add sound effects to a project in GarageBand:

▶   Drag them from the loop browser and arrange or edit as needed.

▶   Trigger them with a MIDI device and record them in a Software Instrument track.

In the next series of exercises, you'll try both methods.

Adding Sound Effects from the Loop Browser

Your goal is to find and add sound effects to enhance the drama of the German Shepherd's crime fighter snapshot, and to apply a siren to the Labrador's rescuer snapshot.

1   Press Command-L to show the loop browser, if it is not already showing.

2   Click the Podcast Sounds button to open the podcast sounds view.

3   In the category column, select Sound Effects. Then select All Effects in the right column.

As you can see, the results list has 176 sound effects. Let's narrow the search using the search field at the bottom of the loop browser.

Since we are looking for something dramatic, let's start with the word *drama* to see what comes up.

4   Type *drama* in the search field and press Return.

That search conveniently narrows the results list to one choice. The upside of having only one choice is that it will either work, or won't. You won't have to spend a lot of time weighing your options on this one.

5   Preview Dramatic Accent 01 in the results list.

It sounds as though it would work for a police dog. The only way to know for sure is to add it to the timeline and see what happens. Don't worry about placing it in the exact spot. Because the sound effect loop will be on its own track, you can always reposition the loop once it is in the timeline.

6   Move the playhead to the beginning of the 12th measure (12.1.1.001).

7   Drag the Dramatic Accent 01 loop from the loop browser to the empty space below the last track in the timeline and release it at the playhead position.

A Textures track appears in the timeline, with the Dramatic Accent 01 region at the playhead position in the new track.

8   Press the Spacebar to hear the new region with the other tracks.

This is definitely the wrong position for the sound effect, but the region itself will probably work if we move it. Let's zoom in and move it so that the Dramatic Accent 01 sound starts right when the words *German Shepherd* flash onscreen.

9   Drag the timeline's zoom slider so that it's around two-thirds of the way to the right. Press the Left Arrow key several times to move the playhead to 11.2.1.001.

10   Drag the Dramatic Accent 01 loop left until it starts at the playhead position.

NOTE ▶ When you are moving a loop in the timeline, be sure to drag anywhere but the very edge so that you are repositioning it instead of extending or trimming it.

11 Play the loop in the timeline.

Much better. In fact, the sound effect works so well that you'd think it was planned all along. The only downside is that the new dramatic loop is a little too loud, which might make it come across as annoying rather than clever.

12 Drag the Textures track volume slider toward the left to around –6.7. Then play the track to hear the dramatic loop at a lower level.

You'll learn more about mixing track levels in Lesson 6, "Mixing Music and Effects." For now, it's just good to know how to adjust an individual track's volume as needed.

Now let's repeat some of the previous steps to add a siren sound effect to the Labrador's snapshot.

13 In the loop browser, type *siren* in the search field and press Return.

The Sound Effects category includes three siren sounds. To see the full names of all three loops you can widen the Name column.

14 Drag the right edge of the Name column header toward the right until you can read the full name of all the loops.

15 Preview each of the siren sounds.

Though the Labrador is shown in front of a fire engine, the Police Car Siren Passing is the clear choice, so it's time to take a little sound-design artistic license and use it anyway.

16 Drag the zoom slider to the left until you can see all of the regions in the timeline.

17 Move the playhead to the beginning of the 15th measure (15.1.1.001). Then drag the Police Car Siren Passing loop from the loop browser to the empty space below the Textures track and release it at the playhead position.

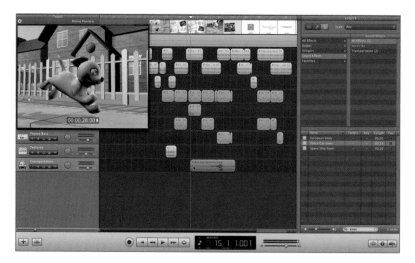

A new Transportation track appears and includes the Police Car Siren Passing loop in the timeline.

18 Play the Police Car Siren Passing loop in the timeline.

Great sound effect, but it takes a while to get going and the actual *passing* of the siren doesn't happen until two dogs later, which is completely wrong for this sound effect. We'll need to trim and move the loop to get the desired effect.

Trimming Sound Effects in the Timeline

Once a sound effect is in the timeline, it's easy to trim the effect and move it to the proper location. In this exercise you'll trim the beginning of the Police Car Siren Passing region and move it. Then you'll add a barking-dog sound effect and trim it so that it works for the final TouchPets Dogs graphic at the end of the trailer. You trim sound effect loops just as you trim any other region, by dragging the lower-left or lower-right edge. You can also split the region at the playhead position and simply delete the unwanted portion. For this exercise you'll try both methods.

As you work with these two sound effects, you'll discover that a sound effect, unlike music, is often positioned according to criteria such as the occurrence of an event within the sound effect itself.

Let's start by moving the region into position.

1 Press the Right Arrow key to move the playhead to the beginning of the 16th measure (16.1.1.001).

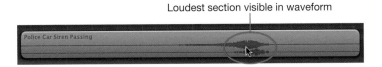

Loudest section visible in waveform

The loudest part of the sound effect will appear as the fattest part of the waveform visible in the Real Instrument loop. Your goal is to move the loudest section of the Police Car Siren Passing sound effect to the playhead position.

2   Select the region in the Transportation track with the loudest point in the waveform and drag it left until the beginning of the loudest part is at the playhead position.

3   Listen to the siren in its new position.

Much better. Now all we have to do is trim the beginning and end of the region.

4   Drag the lower-left edge of the Police Car Siren Passing region toward the right and trim it to around the beginning of the 15th measure (when the Labrador bounds onscreen).

5 Trim the right edge until it ends around the beginning of the 17th measure. Listen to the trimmed region in the timeline.

Feel free to adjust the position and trim the loop to your taste. It's OK if the siren sound starts just before you see the Labrador appear. That actually works to your advantage because the siren motivates his appearance as a rescue dog.

If you didn't complete all the previous steps, or you'd like to compare your work with mine, save your project and open the project **TouchPetsScore05**.

TIP ▶ If you can't see the waveform clearly enough in the timeline, you can always press Command-E to view it in the editor. You'll work more with trimming a region in the editor in Lesson 5, "Creating an iPhone Ringtone."

6 Move the playhead to the beginning of the 26th measure (26.1.1.001)

This is where the animated dog face in the TouchPets Dogs logo barks twice. For this sound effect, you'll add a barking-dog effect that is way too long, then split and discard the parts that don't work with the video.

7   Press Command-L to open the loop browser if it's not already open. Then
     type *bark* in the search field and press Return.

8   Select the Dogs Barking loop and drag it to the empty space below the last
     track in the timeline.

     Once you've released the loop, a new Animals track appears containing the
     Dogs Barking region. This region includes more than a dozen barks. You
     need only two. If you zoom in a bit to find the exact location of the barks,
     then you can match up two consecutive barks that fit the animation.

9   Drag the zoom slider so that it's around two-thirds of the way to the right.
     Then use the Left Arrow and Right Arrow keys to move the playhead to
     25.3.3.001. (This is where the first animated bark begins.)

10   Move the Dogs Barking loop so that the series of barks near the middle
     of the loop starts at the playhead position. Use the waveform in the Dogs
     Barking region as a guide to see when the barks occur.

11   Play the first few barks at the playhead position.

     Don't worry if they don't fit the video exactly; you can tweak their posi-
     tion after you delete all the remaining barks. In fact, now is as good a time
     as any to split the region and delete the unwanted sections.

12 Move the playhead to 25.3.1.001. This should be an area before the first bark you will be using. Select the Dogs Barking loop, if it's not already selected.

13 Press Command-T, or choose Edit > Split, to split the selected region at the playhead position.

14 Press the Right Arrow key to move the playhead to the space between the second and third barks (25.4.3.001). Press Command-T to split the selected region after the second bark.

When you're finished, you should have three separate regions in the Animals track.

15 Click the empty space below the Animals track to deselect all regions in the timeline. Otherwise you might end up deleting everything in the Animals track by mistake.

16 Select the first region in the Animals track and press Delete. Repeat this step with the third region.

17 Play your edited Dogs Barking region in the timeline. Adjust the position if needed.

That's it. In a matter of minutes you found, added, placed, and trimmed two sound effects to enhance the soundtrack. Great work. If you didn't complete all the previous steps, and you want to hear the dog barks already edited in the timeline, open **TouchPetsScore05a**.

Playing and Recording Sound Effects

The sound effects that come with GarageBand are also MIDI samples, which means that you can trigger them with a MIDI instrument, onscreen keyboard, or Musical Typing, and record them as needed into a track. This technique is very useful if you're doing a radio show or podcast and want to trigger a sound effect such as applause, laughter, or a rim shot at the touch of a key. It also comes in handy if you prefer to *play* a sound effect to time it to onscreen action rather than try to find one and edit it to fit.

In this exercise you'll play and record a rim-shot-type drum fill to kick off the trailer music, as well as a cartoon timpani drum sound when one of the pups kicks a ball against a fence.

To record sound effects in the timeline, let's begin by creating the track and assigning the track instrument as Comedy Sounds. If you didn't complete the previous exercises, feel free to open the project **TouchPetsScore05a** to catch up.

1   Choose Track > New Track. In the New Track dialog, select Software
    Instrument as the track type, then click Create.

    A Grand Piano Software Instrument track appears below the Animals
    track in the timeline.

2   In the Track Info pane, select Sound Effects as the track instrument cat-
    egory and Comedy Noises as the specific track instrument.

    The new track changes to Comedy Noises in the timeline.

3   Choose Window > Musical Typing.

    The Musical Typing window appears. If you have an external MIDI key-
    board, feel free to use it for this exercise. Rearrange the Movie Preview and
    Musical Typing windows as needed so that you can see both at the same
    time, as well as the Comedy Noises track at the bottom of the timeline.

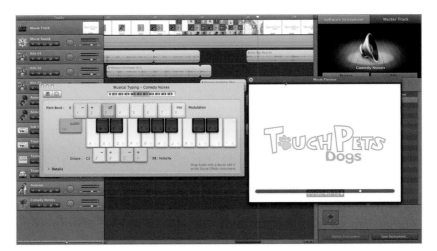

4 Click the keys on the Musical Typing window or press the corresponding keys on your computer keyboard to hear the preassigned comedy noises.

The W key triggers the drum fill sound that you will be using, and the E key triggers the cartoon timpani sound you will record shortly.

5 Move the playhead to the beginning of the 3rd measure (3.1.1.001). This is about 1 measure before you need to trigger the W key (rim shot).

Practice clicking or pressing the W key to trigger just the first part of the drum fill, without the cymbal crash at the end. If the drum part were vocalized as "ta-dum-chhhh," you'd want just the "ta-dum."

Practice once with the video. Start playback, and when you hear the end of the ascending xylophone notes during the Stumptown Game Machine graphic, click or press W to record the "ta-dum."

TIP ▶ You can watch the waveform in the orange TouchPetsMOCKUP region in the Movie Sound track to see where the ascending xylophone sound ends and your "ta-dum" should begin.

Let's try recording the drum part into the track.

NOTE ▶ You'll probably want to turn off the metronome (Command-U) before you start recording, if it is on.

6 Move the playhead back to 3.1.1.001. Make sure that the Comedy Noises track is selected.

7 Click the Record button to start recording. When you hear the end of the ascending xylophone notes during the Stumptown Game Machine graphic, click or press W to record the "ta-dum." Release the W when you're finished and press the Spacebar to stop recording.

Don't worry if the "ta-dum" drum fill that you recorded doesn't line up perfectly before the intro percussion. You can always move it in the time-line. If you really hate your recording, you can press Command-Z to undo the recording and try again.

The green recorded region contains one dash that represents the single note event.

8   Move the playhead to 3.4.3.001, then move the recorded Comedy Noises region in the timeline until the note (not the region) starts at the playhead position.

9   Play the beginning of the project to hear the drum fill as it starts the per-cussion score. Press Command-S to save your progress.

Sounds great. As you can see, recording an effect is as easy and flexible as dragging one from the loop browser. In fact, this method was even better because you didn't have to trim unwanted portions of the effect. If you didn't complete the recording, or would like to hear a completed version, open **TouchPetsScore05b**.

Project Tasks

Now that you know how to record the effects as you play them, you're ready to try one on your own. This time, you'll record the comedy timpani sound around the end of the 9th measure, when the little Labrador puppy hits the ball.

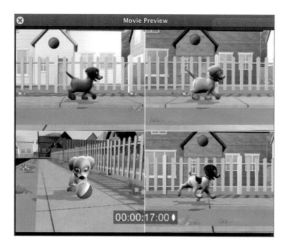

For this effect you can start recording early and just press or click E when you see the dog hit the ball. Stop recording when you're finished.

Don't worry if you trigger the sound late—that's expected, because there will be a lag between the moment when you see the action and when you press the key. When you're finished, simply move the recording earlier until it coincides with the action. Then save your progress.

TIP ▸ The more familiar you are with the footage, the easier it will be for you to record the sound effects to the timeline.

Customizing a Sound Effects Track Instrument

If you liked recording the sound effects by pressing keys, you'll probably also like manually designing your own track instrument. GarageBand lets you assign any effect or loop to any key. Once you've customized the instrument, you can save it for use in other projects. Let's create a comedy sound instrument you can use to add sound effects to the other sections of the video. This exercise will use many of the skills you've developed in previous lessons.

If you didn't complete the previous exercises, feel free to open the project **TouchPetsScore05c** to catch up.

1   Create a new Software Instrument track.

A default Grand Piano Software Instrument track appears.

2   In the Track Info pane, select Sound Effects, Applause and Laughter as the instrument. Then click the Edit tab to access the generator and effects menus.

3   In the Edit pane, set the Sound Effects preset pop-up menu to Manual.

You can now manually assign any loop, stinger, jingle, or sound effect to the keys in the Musical Typing window for your comedy track.

4   Show the Musical Typing window, if it is not already open, and move it so that it isn't blocking any of the Track Info pane.

5   Click the keys on the Musical Typing window to hear the preset.

The default sounds assigned to the instrument should be the Applause and Laughter sound effects. You'll need to use one of the applause sounds shortly, so we'll leave them intact for now. We'll cover some of the laughter sounds with a bark to use with the Jack Russell politician and find a science fiction sound to go with the dachshund scientist.

NOTE ▸ If your default sound effects are not the applause and laughter sounds, change the preset for the Sound Generator from Manual to Applause and Laughter.

6   Press Command-L to show the loop browser.

7   In the podcast sounds view, select Sound Effects as the category and Animals as the subcategory.

8   Drag the Bark effect from the results list to the H key on the Musical Typing keyboard. A green circle with a plus sign (+) indicates you are adding a sound.

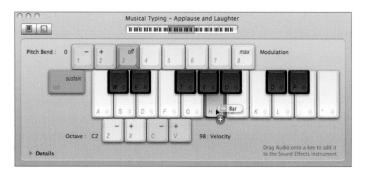

9   Press the H key on your computer keyboard.

The Bark sound effect plays.

10   Move the pointer over the H key on the Musical Typing window.

A yellow help tag appears, showing you the sound assigned to that key.

11 In the loop browser, select the Sci-Fi subcategory in Sound Effects, locate the Warp Engineering 03 effect, and preview it.

This sound will be perfect for the dachshund scientist's snapshot.

12 Drag Warp Engineering 03 from the loop browser to the J key on the Musical Typing window.

Perfect. You now have the applause, bark, and sci-fi sounds needed to finish the sound effects for the score. You can always change what is assigned to a key or add more sounds later.

Saving a Customized Track Instrument

Once you've manually customized your sound effects track instrument, you can save it the same way you save other customized track effects in the Track Info pane.

1 Press Command-I to open the Track Info pane.

The Edit pane should still be showing for the Grand Piano track (customized with comedy noises). If not, click the Edit tab, and select the Grand Piano track at the bottom of the timeline.

2 At the bottom of the Track Info pane, click the Save Instrument button.

The Save Instrument dialog appears.

3 Type your name, followed by *SoundFX*, in the "Save as" field, then click Save.

Your custom comedy track instrument appears in the instrument list in the Track Info pane. It also appears in the track header and Musical Typing window.

Once you've saved an instrument, you can access it for any of your GarageBand projects. You can also modify it by selecting the instrument, dragging different sounds to the keys of the Musical Typing window, then saving the modified version of the instrument.

4   Press Command-I to hide the Track Info pane.

Your new sound effects instrument is ready to play. Before you move on to the next lesson, take a few minutes and experiment with adding other effects to the project.

Project Tasks

Now that you have all the skills you need to play and record sound effects, let's go ahead and record the last three effects. You'll record all three effects to the new SoundFX track using your customized instrument.

Practice each part before you record. When you are ready, do the following:

▶   Record the Bark sound (H) for the Jack Russell terrier. Start recording around the end of the 12th measure (also the end of the German Shepherd part).

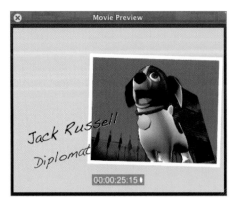

▶ If you don't get it perfect, try again, or just move the barks into position. Yes, the bark is a little big and deep for such a small dog; however, you'll learn how to change his pitch with a filter in Lesson 6, "Mixing Music and Effects."

▶ Record applause from the W key for the Westie on the red carpet. Start recording around the beginning of the 17th measure, then press the W key when the Westie goes from the sidewalk to the walk of fame.

▶ Record the Warp Engineering sound (J) when the dachshund goes from scratching to scientist. Start recording around the beginning of the 19th measure (after the Westie). Press J when the snapshot is taken.

Since the last two clips are right after each other, you could record both in the same region.

Feel free to experiment with other musical parts, effects, and jingles to vary the piece. Have fun! Don't forget to save your finished project.

Open the project **TouchPets05d** if you'd like to hear the finished recorded parts.

Archiving a Project

The last thing you'll do when you finish a score is save an archived version of the project. Archiving a project means that the movie file and the Real Instrument Apple Loops will be saved as part of the project file so that the project can be exported to another Mac.

1   Choose File > Save As.

2   When the dialog opens, select the Archive Project checkbox.

NOTE ▸ If you finished this project using one of the catch-up projects, the Archive Project option may be grayed out. The Archive Project feature is available only if you have added a new recording, Real Instrument loop, or movie to the project.

3   If necessary, select the My GarageBand Projects folder from the Where menu. Click Save.

Congratulations! You finished a draft score for this fun game trailer and learned some handy arranging techniques along the way. Now you have all the skills to create your own interesting scores.

Don't forget to check out the finished trailer that was scored by Ed Bogas, of Bogas Productions, at http://touchpets.ngmoco.com. A copy of the trailer movie with the final production score is also in the Lesson_04 folder; it's titled **TouchPetsTrailer.mov**.

Lesson Review

1. Where do you access movies to add to a project?

2. How many movies can you add to a movie track?

3. How do you duplicate a region within the timeline?

4. How do you transpose, or change the pitch of, a region?

5. When you finish a GarageBand project that includes a movie file, how do you save it so the movie is included with the file?

Answers

1. You can add movies from the Media Browser to a GarageBand project.

2. A movie track can hold only one movie at a time.

3. You can duplicate a region in the timeline by using the Copy and Paste commands or by Option-dragging it.

4. You can transpose a region by selecting it first, then dragging the pitch for that region in the editor.

5. Select the Archive Project checkbox in the Save As dialog to save Real Instrument regions and movie files with the project.

5

Lesson Files   GarageBand09_Book_Files > Lesson_05 > VoiceRingtoneStart

Time   This lesson takes approximately 30 minutes to complete.

Goals   Create a loops-based ringtone

      Record a Software Instrument part

      Play the onscreen music keyboard

      Send a ringtone to iTunes

      Edit a Real Instrument voice track

      Edit regions in the editor

      Merge Real Instrument regions

Creating an iPhone Ringtone

GarageBand includes a project preset that makes it easier than ever to create your own iPhone ringtone. In fact, this process is so simple that you're going to make two different ringtones. In the first exercise, you'll open a project template and record a new Software Instrument part to go with the prebuilt music. Then you'll open a ringtone project that contains a vocal recording and edit the recording to create a fun ringtone.

Opening a Ringtone Template

You can turn any short piece of music or dialogue into an iPhone ringtone.
That includes snippets of your favorite songs. Rather than create a ringtone
from scratch, let's start by opening a ringtone project preset, and then choose
a ringtone template.

1   Open GarageBand. In the New Project dialog, click iPhone Ringtone.

There are three ringtone templates: Example Ringtone, Loops, and Voice.

2   Double-click Loops to create a loops-based ringtone.

3   In the New Project from Template dialog, name the project *LoopRing*, and
save it to the My GarageBand Projects folder on your desktop.

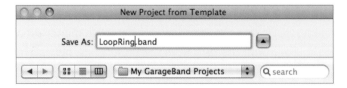

The GarageBand LoopRing project opens with everything you need
already in place to finish and send the ringtone, including a yellow cycle

region above the timeline, the loop browser showing so that you can select additional loops, and a timeline with four tracks already containing a basic Apple Loops arrangement for the ringtone.

4 Play the project to hear the default arrangement.

Sounds good, has a fun electronic feel, and would likely turn heads (in a good way) if it plays in a crowded restaurant. However, it would be even better if you recorded an additional part to add your own distinctive sound to the music.

Recording a New Software Instrument Part

Now that your project is set up, it's time to start recording an additional part. In this exercise, you'll record a synth part to complete the ringtone song. Don't worry if you aren't a musician; you'll still be able to play along and record.

There are three ways to play a Software Instrument in GarageBand.

▶ Connect a MIDI or USB MIDI keyboard to the computer and play the keys on the keyboard. (You can find instructions for connecting a keyboard in Lesson 1.)

▶ Use Musical Typing to turn your computer's keyboard into a musical instrument. (You can try this method in Lesson 2.)

▶ Use the onscreen music keyboard in GarageBand to click the keyboard keys with your mouse.

Playing the Onscreen Music Keyboard

One option for playing music with GarageBand is the onscreen music keyboard. You can use the keyboard to both play and record Software Instruments. First, let's create a new Software Instrument track that you'll use to record your part.

1 Choose Track > New Track, then select Software Instrument from the New Track dialog. Click Create.

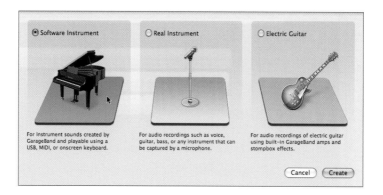

A new Grand Piano track appears below the other tracks in the timeline. Grand Piano is the default Software Instrument; however, you can change it at any time to a different Software Instrument.

2 To show the onscreen music keyboard, choose Window > Keyboard.

The onscreen music keyboard appears, ready to play the selected Grand Piano track.

NOTE ▶ The onscreen music keyboard works only for Software Instrument tracks.

3 Drag the lower-right corner of the keyboard down and to the right to resize it for larger keys that are easier to click.

TIP ▶ The onscreen music keyboard is touch sensitive. Click the top of the keys to play with a lighter velocity and get a quieter sound. Click the bottom of the keys to play with a harder velocity and get a louder sound. You can always change the velocity of Software Instrument notes in the editor after they've been recorded.

4   Play the onscreen keyboard by clicking the notes on the keyboard.

Although you can play music this way, it's not the easiest way to create complex music arrangements. However, it will work perfectly for this ring-tone composition.

Let's change the track instrument to a synth sound that works better for this project.

5   On the Track Info pane, choose Synth Leads as the instrument category (left column) and Solo Star as the instrument.

6   Click a few notes to hear the Solo Star instrument in action.

The part you'll play will be incredibly simple. Because the project is in the key of C, you'll simply click the C key (marked C2—usually the first key on a standard keyboard, including the onscreen music keyboard) and drag the pointer toward the right until you reach the C3 key, an octave higher. Then you'll do it again starting with the C3 key and dragging toward the right to C4.

Your goal is to play and hold C2 for the 3rd and 4th measures, and then drag to C3 during the 5th measure. Hold the C3 note through the 6th measure. Click C3 again and hold through the 7th and 8th measures, and then drag to C4 during the 9th measure. Hold the C4 note until the 10th measure.

7   Practice clicking C2 and dragging across the white keys to C3. Then do it again from C3 to C4. Try again while the song is playing. Choose Control > Metronome, or press Command-U to turn off the metronome during your recording.

Don't worry if you miss a key along the way, or overshoot the last note and backtrack. Whatever you do will sound fine in this composition. When you're ready, go ahead and try recording.

8   Press C to turn off the cycle region for this recording. Press Return to move the playhead to the beginning of the project.

9   Press R to start recording, and play your part. When you're finished, press the Spacebar to stop recording.

Play back your recording. If you're happy, continue finishing the ringtone. If not, press Command-Z to undo and try again.

10 Press Command-S to save your project.

Nice work. If you happen to hear that same tune with the Synth Riff as a ringtone somewhere, give that person a high five for going through the same exercise as you. Or better yet, show off your own custom ringtone. It's only a matter of time before ringtones have their own awards.

Sending a Ringtone to iTunes

When you've finished building your ringtone song, the last step is to create a cycle region the same duration as the song. That way you can hear it loop as it will when the phone rings. Then you can send the finished ringtone to iTunes.

1 Press C to show the cycle region. Resize the cycle region so that it ends at the 11th measure (or at the end of the last region in the timeline.)

2 Choose Share > Send Ringtone to iTunes.

The finished LoopRing ringtone plays in iTunes and is ready to sync to your iPhone. You'll learn more about setting GarageBand preferences for iTunes and sharing your projects in Lesson 8, "Sharing Your Projects."

3 Press Command-Q to quit iTunes.

4   Press Command-W to close the LoopRing project.

5   If necessary, click No in the "save with iLife preview" dialog.

> **NOTE ▶** GarageBand adds effects, including special compressors, to ring-
> tone projects to maximize the quality of the sound through an iPhone
> speaker when the phone rings.

Editing a Real Instrument Voice Track

In the next lesson, you'll work with vocal recordings for a podcast project. In
this exercise, you'll edit a Real Instrument vocal region to make a special ringtone that was created as a Valentine's Day present. You can apply this exercise's
techniques to your own voice recordings, whether they're voiceover, dialogue,
or a special voice ringtone for whatever occasion you choose.

1   Open the project **VoiceRingtoneStart** in the Lesson_05 folder. Then choose
    File > Save As and save it to the My GarageBand Projects folder on your
    desktop.

2   Play the project to hear the finished Valentine's Day ringtone. Imagine
    hearing this ringtone in a crowded elevator. When you stop laughing,
    pause playback.

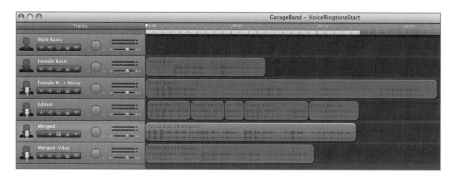

For this project, I started with the Voice ringtone template, and then changed
the track instrument to Female Narrator Noisy to apply the noise-reduction
filter automatically to the track. I used the built-in microphone on my lap-
top, so the recording was extra noisy.

NOTE ▶ You can record vocals with professional microphones connected to an audio interface, a USB microphone such as the Blue Snowball, or even an iSight microphone. Make sure that you choose the correct input source for your microphone in System Preferences before recording in GarageBand.

In this case, the "female narrator" is my two-and-a-half-year-old daughter, Katie. We decided to surprise my husband, Klark, with a ringtone on Valentine's morning.

This project includes the before and after versions of the edited recordings.

The top Female Basic track includes the initial recording. The Female Narrator Noisy track includes a second, longer recording.

The Edited track is the result of removing all of the unwanted parts of the recordings and arranging the rest of the regions in the track.

The Merged track consists of one merged region that was created from all of the edited parts.

The Merged-Vday track is the same as the Merged, except that I removed the "Happy Valentine's Day, Daddy" from the beginning so it can be used as a ringtone beyond the month of February.

3   Mute the Merged track and solo the Female Basic track to hear the first recording.

You can see the waveform pretty clearly in this region, so you can trim the beginning and ending right in the timeline.

4   Drag the timeline's zoom Zoom slider toward the right (about two-thirds
    of the way across the slider control) until you have a really clear view of
    the waveform and region in the timeline.

    Your goal with this timeline editing is to remove most of the silence
    (straight horizontal lines) at the beginning and end of the region.

5   Drag the lower-left corner of the Female Basic region in the Female
    Basic track toward the right until you get close to the beginning of the
    waveform.

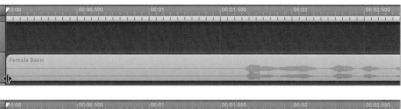

6   Scroll down the timeline until you see the last half of the region.

7   Drag the right edge of the region toward the left to trim off the excess
    recording. Be sure to stop trimming when you get close to the waveform.

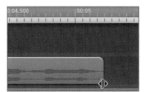

8   Press C to hide the cycle region. Play the trimmed region to make sure it
    sounds OK. If you accidentally trimmed some of the words, drag the lower
    corner outward to reveal the missing waveform.

    Unfortunately, Katie had a cold the day we recorded this, so the effects will
    eventually filter out some of the noise, but not the lovely nasal tones.

9   Unsolo the Female Basic track and solo the Female Narrator Noisy track.

10 Press Command-S to save your progress.

Now that you've seen how easy it is to edit a voice recording in the timeline, let's try editing within the region. For that more advanced maneuver, you'll need to work in the editor.

Editing Regions in the Editor

The editor allows you to see a much larger, more focused view of regions, making it easier to pinpoint areas that need editing. In the timeline edit that you performed in the previous exercise, you trimmed away the parts that you didn't want. Your goal in this exercise is to select and remove all of the sections of the recording that you don't want to keep. Mainly it's me trying to direct Katie to say what I wanted her to say.

To open the editor, you can either click the Editor button (which looks like scissors cutting a waveform) or double-click the region that you want to edit.

1   Double-click the Female Basic region in the Female Narrator Noisy track to open it in the editor.

The editor appears at the bottom of the GarageBand window.

2   Drag the editor's zoom slider to around one-third from the left for a good zoom level for this type of work. Feel free to zoom in more or less as needed.

3   Press Return to move the playhead to the beginning of both the editor and the timeline. Then play the project and watch the waveform in the editor as it plays.

You should be able to hear the parts that need to be removed from the region.

To select part of a region in the editor, you drag to highlight the area. Once you've made a selection, you click the selection to make it a separate region. Once the separate region is selected, you simply delete it from the project. Let's try it.

4   Play from the beginning and pause after Katie says, "Happy Valentine's Day, Daddy." (Just beyond 3 seconds in the ruler at the top of the editor.)

5   Click the crosshair cursor on the middle of the region in the editor, and continue holding down the mouse button while you drag right to create a selection. Release the mouse button just after 6 seconds in the ruler. (Just before the waveform where Katie talking starts again.)

> **TIP** Press the Spacebar after you make a selection in the editor to hear that selection. If you don't like your selection, undo and try again.

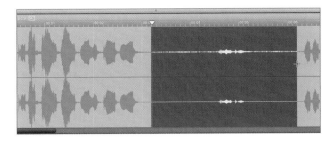

6 Press Delete to remove the selection from the region.

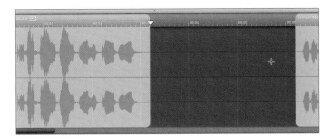

NOTE ▶ Clicking the selected area turns it into a separate region but does not delete it.

As you can see, it's pretty easy to select and delete specific areas of a region within the editor.

Project Tasks

Now it's your turn to remove the rest of the unwanted audio from the track. Scroll down through the region in the editor, and delete any of the sections that shouldn't be there. Don't forget to trim off the nasty pop at the end. When you're finished, you should have four separate regions in the Female Narrator Noisy track. Save your progress before moving on to the next section.

Merging Real Instrument Regions

The final steps to completing this ringtone are to arrange the regions and merge them into one finished region. Technically you don't have to merge them, but doing so ensures that you don't have space between regions. Merging regions is often used with music recordings to create a finished track or section that can then be looped or duplicated more easily as a single region.

1   Press Command-E to hide the editor if it's still showing. Drag the timeline's zoom slider about halfway to the right to match the screenshots.

2   Drag the second and third regions in the Female Narrator Noisy track toward the left until they're all touching each other in the Timeline. Feel free to overlap them slightly to cover excess silence at the end of a region.

3   Move the trimmed region from the Female Basic track down to the space between the third and fourth regions in the Female Narrator Noisy track.

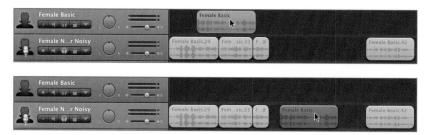

4   Move the last two regions in the track toward the left until all of the regions are next to each other in the track. Feel free to use the Edited track below as a guide for placement.

5   Double-click the track header to select all of the regions within the Female Narrator Noisy track.

6   Choose Edit > Join, or press Command-J to join the regions.

The region appears as a single merged region in the track.

7   Trim the pop from the beginning of the region in either the timeline or the editor.

8   Save the finished project.

That's it! You've edited a voice recording in both the timeline and the editor. You can use these techniques to edit your own recordings in the future. If you want to complete this ringtone, simply solo the track that you want to use, create a cycle region the length of the region so that it loops properly, and then choose Share > Send Ringtone to iTunes.

Lesson Review

1.   What types of ringtone templates are available?

2.   Where can you edit Real Instrument regions?

3.   When you hear a region of your song that needs to be removed, how do you isolate it?

4.   What is a benefit of merging Real Instrument regions?

Answers

1.   GarageBand comes with three ringtone templates: Example Ringtone, Loops, and Voice.

2.   You can edit a Real Instrument region in the timeline or the editor.

3.   In the editor, drag to highlight the area. Once you've made a selection, you click the selection to make it a separate region. Then select it and press Delete to remove it.

4.   You can create a finished track or section that can then be looped or duplicated more easily as a single region.

6

Time This lesson takes approximately 60 minutes to complete.

Goals Work with the arrange track

Create a basic mix

Balance volume levels on individual tracks

Pan tracks

Add effects to a track and the overall song

Work with volume and pan automation curves

Dynamically pan a track

Work with the master track

Work with ducking

Lesson 6
Mixing Music and Effects

As you learned in Lesson 3, you can record and create professional-quality music with GarageBand. However, to make your finished songs actually sound professional, you need to understand the fine art of mixing music.

In Lesson 4, you arranged a song in the timeline using basic and advanced music arrangement techniques. Your goal in this lesson is to take an arranged song to the next level to make it sound like a professional composition. To accomplish this, you'll need to apply professional mixing techniques, including balancing the volume, panning tracks, fixing the timing, and adding effects. Along the way, you'll also learn some handy shortcuts for features you're already familiar with.

The good news is that you won't need any external mixing hardware or interfaces to achieve all of these goals. GarageBand includes an easy-to-use track mixer with controls for volume level and pan position.

Creating a Basic Mix

Mixing a song is the art of carefully blending all of the different sounds and musical textures into one cohesive, balanced piece of music. Arranging regions in separate tracks is easy once you get the hang of it. Mixing takes a little more practice and some training. If you have a pair of stereo headphones (even those from an iPod), you should use them now. Great external computer speakers also work well.

> **TIP** ▶ Before you mix a song in GarageBand, it's a good idea to check the volume level of your computer. If you have a professionally recorded CD or song in iTunes, play a song and adjust your computer's volume levels to your liking before continuing.

When mixing, you start with a rough (basic) mix, then fine-tune the mix, and finally polish the mix in the final master. There are six basic steps for creating the final mix:

1   Make sure that the song is indeed finished, and that all parts have been recorded, added, and arranged.

2   Find and fix any musical imperfections in timing, tempo, or performance. (This may require editing or rerecording a section of the song.)

3   Adjust the volume levels of the individual tracks to balance the sounds of the different instruments.

4   Adjust the pan positions of the individual tracks to place the sounds in the correct locations in the stereo field.

5   Add and adjust effects to enhance the sounds of individual tracks or the whole song.

6   Create dynamic volume and pan changes over time using the volume and pan automation curves on individual tracks and on the master track.

Adjusting the Tempo

Before you can make any mixing decisions, it's a good idea to listen to the song. For this lesson, you'll be mixing a variation of a song in the Roots Rock genre created in Magic GarageBand.

1   Open **RootsRockStart** from the Lesson_06 folder and start playback.

As you play the song, listen for the following:

► Are some parts difficult to hear? Do some parts seem too loud? Is the overall volume of the song even?

► Does the song sound and feel finished?

What was your impression of the unmixed song? The tempo seems a bit slow. All of the musical elements (instruments and parts) are there, but the levels are all over the place. The unmixed song doesn't sound or feel very professional.

Stepping up the tempo of the piece is easy, so let's go ahead and take care of it before moving on and saving the project. *Tempo* is pacing—the pulse or speed of the song—and it affects how the song sounds and feels. Software Instruments and Apple Loops automatically change tempo to match the project.

The current tempo is 75 beats per minute, which we've already established feels a bit slow. A tempo of 85 ought to be fast enough to pick up the pace without it feeling like the band is in a hurry or drank too much coffee.

2   In the LCD, click the current tempo (75) and drag the slider up to 85.

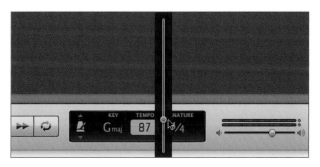

NOTE ▶ If the tempo is not showing, click the left icon of the LCD and choose the Project mode.

3   Play the song again at the new tempo.

Much better. Too bad you can't actually change the tempo of a live performance that easily.

TIP ▶ If you are planning to record a part that is difficult to play, or that needs to be played faster than you can physically play it, record the part at a slower tempo, then speed up the project's tempo after you're done recording.

4   Choose File > Save As, and save the project in the My GarageBand Projects folder on your desktop.

If you didn't create a folder in the previous lessons, click the New Folder button in the Save As dialog and create a folder where you can save your mixing project.

Now that you have step 2 out of the way and have fixed the song's tempo, let's take care of step 1 and finish the song. In this case, the song is only a minute and a half in length, and the client needs it to be closer to 2 minutes, if possible.

Using the Arrange Track

If you listen to most songs, you'll realize that they're usually arranged in distinct sections, such as introduction, verse, and chorus. The arrange track makes it easier to see these parts of your song and makes it simple to move, duplicate, or delete sections at any time.

In this exercise, you'll use the arrange track to quickly duplicate a section of the song to extend the overall length of the piece. The arrange track appears at the top of the window below the beat ruler.

1   Click the Chorus arrange region located at the top of the GarageBand window.

NOTE ▸ If the arrange track isn't visible, choose Track > Show Arrange Track.

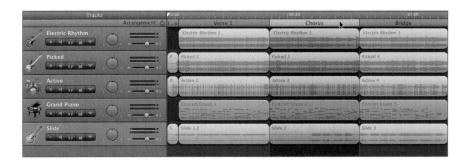

The Chorus arrange region darkens to show that it's been selected.

2   Hold down the Option key and drag toward the right to create a cloned version of the section. Place the Chorus copy region between Verse 2 and the Outro sections.

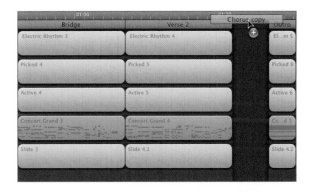

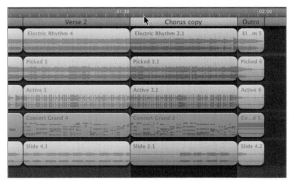

Because the song's chorus is the same part, you can change the name to remove the word *copy* from the second chorus.

3   Double-click the Chorus copy arrange region's title. Change the title for the region to *Chorus.*

4   Play the last half of the song to hear the modified ending.

Well, it's almost there. The song is indeed longer, but the lead guitar in the Slide track cuts off abruptly as the song progresses from Verse 2 to the chorus. Fortunately, there is an easy fix. You can simply duplicate the piece of slide guitar in the Outro region and place it at the beginning of the second chorus.

5   Option-drag the Slide section in the Outro region and place the duplicate copy at the beginning of the second Chorus section.

Make sure that you place the duplicate over the silence at the beginning of the chorus and do not overlap the end of the Verse 2 region. If you make a mistake, Choose Edit > Undo and try again.

6   Play that section again to hear the finished arrangement. When you are done, press Command-S to save your progress.

TIP ▶ To add a new region, click the plus sign in the track header area of the arrange track.

Working with the Track Mixer

It is essential to have a basic understanding of the track mixer so that you can effectively mix the song. The track mixer is located between the track header and the timeline.

Pan dial   Level meter

Volume slider

Adjusting Levels with the Volume Slider

You can adjust the volume level for an individual track with the volume slider. The overall goal is to blend the levels of all the tracks so that all the instruments can be heard but the right tracks are emphasized.

By default, the volume slider is set to 0 dB (decibels) for all tracks. That doesn't mean the volume of the track is 0 decibels. It actually means that there has been no change applied to the track's volume level. This applies whether the track contains recorded regions or loops. You can adjust the volume for an individual track while the playhead is static or while you're playing the song.

In our rock song, there are five tracks. Which levels should you adjust first? Great question. Generally, you prioritize your tracks and start with the lead vocals or lead instruments. Because this song doesn't contain vocals, the slide guitar and piano tracks containing the melody are the lead instruments, and therefore they take priority. Once the levels of the lead tracks are good, you then move on to the rhythm tracks.

Let's start by adjusting the volume level on the Slide track. Before you adjust the volume, you'll need to solo the track so you can hear the level change without the other tracks.

1   Click the Slide Guitar track header to select the track in the timeline.

2   Press S, or click the Solo button, to solo the track.

    The soloed track becomes the only audible track in the timeline.

3   Drag the volume slider all the way to the left.

    The slider turns blue when you click it to indicate that it's been selected. The lowest volume level is −144.0 dB (silence). That means the level has been lowered by 144.0 dB from the original volume level.

    Next, you'll raise the volume while the track is playing. Because you're trying to determine how loud to make the overall track, it's a good idea to play a prominent section of that track.

4   Play the song starting at the Bridge section.

5   Drag the volume slider to the right to raise the volume level while the track is playing. Release the slider when you think you've reached a good volume level. Then pause playback.

How do you know if your volume level is good? You can look at the level meter.

Reading the Level Meter

The level meter uses colored bars to visually represent the volume level for the track.

Average level   Peak level

Clipping indicators

The lower the volume, the shorter the solid colored bars. If the color is green, the level is within a safe range and isn't too loud. If the color turns from green to yellow, that means caution—your sound is bordering on being too loud. If it turns red, you need to stop and turn the volume down immediately. The two circles at the end of the level meter are the clipping indicators. *Clipping* means your music is not only too loud but could also be distorted.

The level meter in GarageBand is *sticky*, which means a single line of the colored bar will stick to the highest position on the meter while the average levels continue to change. The average volume level is marked by the solid colored bar, and the peaks are marked with the vertical line.

> **TIP** If the tracks in the song were professionally recorded—or at least the levels were safe as recorded—it's likely the lead instrument volume levels will end up somewhere near 0 dB on the track mixer meters, because the levels were already good. Remember to record your own tracks with a good solid level on the meters to ensure a great sound and easier mixing.

Checking Combined Levels

Now that you've set the volume level of the Slide track, let's take a moment to find a good level for the Grand Piano track. You'll start by soloing the Grand Piano track and unsoloing the Slide track to find a good level for the piano. Then solo the Slide track again so you can hear both the lead guitar and the piano tracks and make sure the combined levels are good. Play the entire song with the guitar and piano tracks soloed, and watch their level meters. Try a volume level of −2.4 dB for the guitar track and −1.6 dB for the piano track.

Using the Pan Dial

The pan dial controls the left-to-right placement of a track within the stereo field. The *pan* in *pan dial* stands for *panoramic*. A panoramic photograph is an image that includes everything you can see without turning your head. A stereo field is everything you can hear from the far left to the far right without turning your head.

Imagine a panoramic photograph of the Rocky Mountains with a train cutting through the far-left side of the image. Visually, you place the train on the left side of your field of view. You would also place the sound of the train on the far-left side of the stereo field.

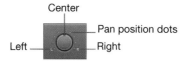

By default, all of the tracks in GarageBand start with the pan position set to the center. With center pan position, the sound is heard equally out of both speakers—it sounds like it's directly in front of you in the center of the audio space.

To adjust the pan position of a track, click the small white dots around the pan dial. Let's adjust the pan position of the selected track.

This exercise works best if you're listening through headphones, so take a minute and put on your headset before you start. Make sure your headphones have the right speaker (R) on the right ear and the left speaker (L) on the left ear.

1   Unsolo the Grand Piano track.

2   On the Slide track, click the dot next to the L on the lower-left side of the pan dial to change the pan position to the far left of the stereo field.

3   Press C to show the cycle region. Press the Spacebar to listen to the cycle region. Feel free to move the cycle region to a different part of the song by dragging from the center of the yellow bar.

Notice that the guitar part sounds like it's coming from the far left.

NOTE ▶ If you hear the guitar coming from the far right, you probably have your headphones on backward.

4   Click the dot next to the R on the lower-right side of the pan dial to change the pan position to the far right of the stereo field.

Notice that the sound of the guitar jumps to the far-right side.

5   Click the dot on the left side that's one dot away from the center position.

If the pan dial were a clock, the dot would be at 11:00.

Notice that the guitar still sounds like it's on the left, but closer to the middle of the stereo field. Now let's add the Grand Piano and make it sound like it's playing on the opposite position from the center of the stage (1:00 on the pan dial).

6   Solo the Grand Piano track so that both the guitar and the piano tracks are soloed.

7   On the Grand Piano track, click the dot on the right side that's one dot away from the center position (1:00). Listen to the panned tracks.

Notice how it sounds like two different musicians sitting on the right-center and left-center of the stage.

8   Press the Spacebar to stop playback. Then press C to hide the cycle region.

NOTE ▸ To quickly reset the volume and pan controls to the default settings, Option-click the controls. The default volume level is 0 dB, and the default pan position is center.

Now that you have a better understanding of the track mixer and how to use it, let's finish mixing the song.

Balancing Volume Levels for Individual Tracks

As you can imagine, there are hundreds of combinations of volume levels you could try on this song. Instead of experimenting, let's use logic and come up with a plan.

To mix volume levels, you need to know what type of sound you're going for in your song. A vocal ballad might favor the vocal tracks and the lead instruments and keep the drums low in the mix. A club song might favor the drums and synth bass tracks and bury the supporting tracks. Rock songs often favor the lead guitar and vocals and keep the drums about midlevel. Every song is different, every style is different, and every mix is different.

The first step is to adjust the volume level of each track as needed to balance the song. Mixing music tracks is very much like mixing cooking ingredients. You start with the main ingredients, like water and tomatoes for a marinara sauce. Then you slowly add more ingredients, tasting along the way to make sure there isn't too much or too little of anything before moving on to the next. Following this analogy, the main ingredients (lead tracks) of the song have already been adjusted. It's time to work on the rhythm tracks, which in this case are Electric Rhythm, Picked (bass), and finally, percussion.

1   Solo the Electric Rhythm track and play it with the other soloed tracks.

Chances are, you'll find the Electric Rhythm guitar part far too dominant in the mix. Not only is it overpowering, but you can't even hear the piano over the rhythm guitar anymore.

2   Lower the Electric Rhythm track to around –8.8 dB. Feel free to raise or lower it to your own liking.

> **TIP** If you aren't sure about an instrument's volume level in the mix, toggle the Solo or Mute button for that instrument's track on and off. If you don't really notice it missing when it isn't playing, the level is probably too low.

Next, you'll add the bass that's in the Picked track. Before you mix the rest of the tracks, it's a good idea to mute the remaining tracks, then unsolo all the soloed tracks. That way you simply unmute the final tracks as you go. There's no sense in soloing all of a song's tracks; that kind of defeats the purpose of solo.

3   Unsolo all three of the soloed tracks (Electric Rhythm, Grand Piano, and Slide).

Press the Up Arrow or Down Arrow key to select the Picked (bass) track and press M to mute the track. Press the Down Arrow key to select the Active (drum) track and press M to mute the track.

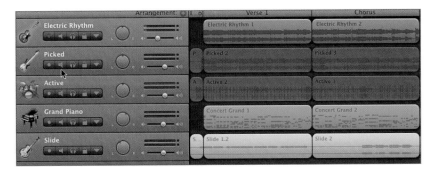

4   Play the song from the beginning. Select the Picked track and press M to unmute the track.

The default volume level (0 dB) is a good starting point for the rhythm guitar. However, you may find it a little too heavy in the mix, which takes away from the lead instruments.

5 Lower the level for the Picked track to around –7.6.

6 Unmute the Active track and listen to the drums in the mix.

How do the drums sound and *feel* with the other tracks? They seem just a little too loud. Remember, your goal isn't to raise the volume of each track to match but to find balance among the tracks.

7 Lower the level of the Active track to around –5.6 dB.

NOTE ▶ Adjusting track volume is like adjusting water temperature in a sink with separate cold and hot controls. If you're running both hot and cold water, and you want to make the overall temperature hotter, you can just turn down the cold instead of turning up the hot. The same goes for volume—instead of making a track louder to hear it better, you might need to turn down the other tracks a bit.

You've completed a basic mix to balance the volume levels of the different tracks, and even panned the lead instruments to distribute their sounds between speakers. Now we'll add a few effects to polish the mix.

Adding Effects to a Track

Effects are the secret to making great-sounding music. They can enhance the sound of individual tracks or an overall song. GarageBand comes fully loaded with professional-quality effects. You can choose from the effects presets included with each Real Instrument and Software Instrument, or customize the effects and save your own preset.

If you didn't finish the previous exercises, open the file **RootsRockMixed** in the Lesson_06 folder to catch up.

Let's add some effects to bring out the Slide track and make the Grand Piano sound really stand out in the mix. You'll start by soloing the track you're working with and creating a cycle region so you can hear how the track sounds before and after we adjust the effects.

1   Select the Slide track and press S to solo the track. Then, press C to open the cycle region.

2   Create a cycle region over the Verse 2 region if the cycle region isn't over that section of the song.

3   Press Command-I or double-click the Slide track header to open the Track Info pane.

4   Click the Edit tab on the Track Info pane to reveal the track's effects.

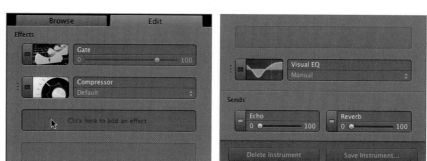

Each track includes gate, compressor, and Visual EQ effects. There are also four empty effects slots. You can click an empty slot and choose an effect.

The two Sends sliders near the bottom of the Track Info pane control the amount of the track's output that is sent to the master echo and reverb effects. Notice the blue LEDs on the Echo and Reverb sends that indicate those effects are active.

For this exercise, you'll use the compressor, which can modify the instruments' frequencies to improve the sound in the mix.

5   Click the LED on the compressor to make it active (blue).

6   Click the presets menu currently set to Default to see the compressor presets, and select Electric Guitar Smoothen.

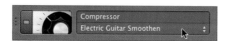

A dialog appears to warn you that you're changing the track's instrument setting. Click Continue.

7   Start playback to hear the sound of the Slide guitar with the new compressor setting. Press S to unsolo the track and hear it with the other tracks. Click the compressor LED to turn off the effect and hear the guitar without it. Click the LED again to turn it back on.

What a difference a little compression can make! The guitar sound really stands out and feels like a lead instrument. In fact, it sounds so good you may want to turn it down a bit in the mix. It isn't uncommon to need to tweak volume levels once effects have been applied.

8   Lower the volume of the Slide track to around –4.8, and then pause playback.

9   Select the Grand Piano track. Press S to solo the selected track. Then turn on the compressor effect for that track in the Track Info pane.

10   Click the Edit button (the rectangle with a graphic) next to the LED to open the manual controls for the current effect.

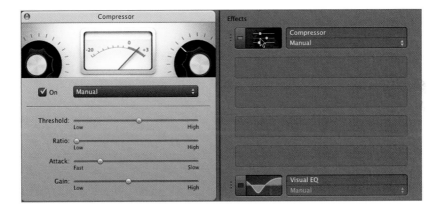

The compressor Preset window appears. You could manually adjust the parameters here, or add a preset. Feel free to experiment with the controls before choosing the preset in the next step.

11 Click the menu in the compressor's Preset window and choose Piano Upfront. Click Continue on the warning dialog, and then listen to the Grand Piano track with the compressor.

12 Unsolo the Grand Piano track and listen to it with the song. When you're finished, hide the cycle region, pause playback, and close the compressor's Preset window.

Once again the results are quite extraordinary. For the first time, you can really hear the piano part in the song, without its stepping all over the lead guitar. As you can plainly hear, the use of effects such as the compressor presets can help your music sound better.

> **NOTE ▶** If you manually adjust an effect, you'll see a dialog asking if you want to save the instrument settings. If you think you'll use those settings again, go ahead and save them.

Adding Effects to the Overall Song

To add an effect to an individual track, you used the Track Info pane for that specific track. The Track Info pane for the master track shows the effects settings for the overall project.

Let's open the Track Info pane for the master track and add an effects preset to the entire song.

1 Press Command-I, or click the Track Info button if it isn't already showing.

2 Click Master Track at the upper-right corner of the Track Info pane to show the master effects.

You can add and modify effects in the Edit pane of the master track just as you work with effects for an individual track. You can also click the Browse tab to choose a preset that fits the song.

3   On the Track Info pane for the master track, click the Browse tab.

4   Select Rock as the master category, then select Rock Basic as the specific master preset. If a dialog appears, click Continue to apply the preset.

5   Continue playback. While the song is playing, press the Down Arrow key to hear the other Rock preset effects applied to the song. Stop playback when you've selected an effect.

Did you find a favorite preset? They all sound good, but the Classic Rock and LA Rock presets stand out. You can select whichever you like best.

NOTE ▸ The master presets are combinations of EQ and compressor effects. You can turn the effects on and off, or modify them under the Edit tab of the Track Info pane, just like the effects applied to a track.

6   Command-I to hide the Track Info pane for the master track.

Now that you've finished your mix and added effects, it's a good idea to update the name of the project.

7   Choose File > Save As and save the project as *RootsRockMixedFX*. Save the project in the My GarageBand Projects folder on your desktop.

Your mix is complete and the song sounds great. You can apply your new mixing skills to your own music.

Preparing the Project

For this exercise, you will work with a song called "Highway Bound." Unlike the previous song, which was created in Magic GarageBand, this song was created and arranged from Apple Loops, with the addition of one recorded Software Instrument track.

You'll see many of the arranging techniques applied to this song that you worked with in Lesson 4. However, it's always nice to work with a variety of songs and music genres as you learn the fine art of mixing music.

1   Save the current project.

2   Choose File > Open. Navigate to your GarageBand09_Book_Files folder on the desktop and choose Lesson_06 > **HighwayBoundFX**.

3   Choose File > Save As, and save a copy of this project in the My GarageBand Projects folder.

4   Play the song to familiarize yourself with the project.

As the music plays, listen to the way the instrument volume levels are carefully mixed. Also, notice the various pan positions of the instruments within the stereo field.

Locking Tracks to Improve Processor Speed

Once the volume and panning levels have been adjusted, it's a good idea to lock the tracks that are finished if a song has a lot of tracks. Track locking serves two primary purposes:

▶   It prevents unwanted changes.

▶   It renders the track to the computer's hard disk, which frees up processing power for the rest of the tracks.

You certainly don't need to lock tracks unnecessarily. However, when you're working with a lot of Software Instrument tracks that require a great deal of processing power, locking tracks and rendering them to the hard disk can improve GarageBand's performance.

Let's lock all of the Drum Kit tracks to free up some of the processing required to play those Software Instrument tracks.

1   On each of the Drum Kit track headers, click the Lock Track button.

The Lock Track button turns green to indicate that the track is locked.

2   Play the song from the beginning to render the locked tracks.

A progress indicator (a moving bar) appears, showing that the tracks are locking and rendering. When rendering is complete, the window closes automatically, and the song plays from the beginning. If you click the Truncate button in the progress window, the rendering will stop at the current playhead position and only that portion of the timeline will be rendered.

NOTE ▶ You can unlock a track anytime by clicking its Lock Track button. If you do unlock a track, any other locked tracks will remain locked and rendered until you unlock them.

That's it. You've rendered those four tracks to the hard disk, which frees up processor speed for effects and other advanced features.

It's time to move on to some more advanced mixing features, which include using automation curves to create dynamic volume and pan changes over time, and working with the master track to apply changes to the overall song.

Working with Volume and Pan Automation Curves

So far, you have adjusted the volume and pan levels for individual tracks by using the controls in the track mixer. This method is great for setting one volume or pan level for an entire track. But what if you want the level to change during the song?

This next series of exercises will show you how to change volume and panning within a track by setting control points along the volume or pan automation curve. To make changes to an automation curve, you first need to show the curve in the timeline.

Showing Volume Curves

There are two ways to show the volume curve for a track:

▶ Press A (for *automation*) to show the volume automation curve for the selected track.

▶ In the track header, click the triangle to the right of the Lock Track button.

Our goal in the next two exercises is to show the volume curve and then set control points on the volume curve to fade the volume of the Hollywood Strings track up and down during the song.

First, you need to show the volume curve.

1   Select the Hollywood Strings track.

2   Click the triangle next to the Lock Track button to show the track's volume curve.

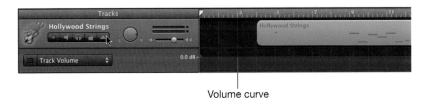

Volume curve

The volume curve appears in the automation row below the Hollywood Strings track.

In this case, the volume curve isn't actually a curve. It's a straight line that represents the steady volume of the track.

3 Drag the Hollywood Strings track volume slider all the way to the left and watch the movement of the volume curve.

As you can see, the volume slider moves the volume curve.

4 Option-click the Hollywood Strings track volume slider to reset the slider to the default position.

If the volume curve does not move to the default position, click the Hollywood Strings track volume slider once to apply the new position to the volume curve.

Adding and Adjusting Control Points

Now that you can see the volume curve, you can make adjustments to it using control points. Control points set a fixed volume level on the volume curve at a specific point along the timeline. Changing the position of a control point allows you to bend the volume curve, which raises or lowers the volume between the control points.

Control points are often used to fade music in or fade music out. Slowly fading the volume of a song up from silence is *fading in* the music; slowly fading the song down to silence is *fading out* the music.

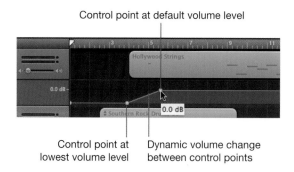

Control point at default volume level

Control point at   Dynamic volume change
lowest volume level   between control points

You need two control points to change the volume dynamically. The first control point is for the starting volume level. The second control point is for the new volume level. You add a new control point by clicking the volume curve. You move a control point by dragging the point.

Let's add some control points to fade in the Hollywood Strings track.

1   Drag the control point at the beginning of the volume curve down to the bottom of the track to lower the volume of the track to the lowest possible volume (silence).

Default volume level

This control point sets the volume for the overall track. Notice the gray horizontal line above the current volume curve position. This line indicates the default volume level.

2   Move the playhead to the beginning of the 5th measure.

NOTE ► You may wish to zoom in to the track one or two levels (Control– Right Arrow) to see the numbered measures you are looking for in the beat ruler.

3   Click the volume curve at the playhead position at the beginning of the 5th measure (bar 5) to set a control point where the first note is played in the Hollywood Strings region.

Track automation pop-up menu

Track automation on/off button

A new control point appears in the volume curve at the playhead position. This control point has a value that is the same as the lowest volume level.

Notice that the pop-up menu in the automation row header is set to Track Volume and that the volume curve is active (the button is colored). The track automation curve turns on automatically whenever you select or create a control point in the curve. You can turn the track curve on or off by clicking the square button to the left of the pop-up menu. If you turn on either the track volume or pan curve, they both become activated and both the volume slider control and the pan dial are deactivated.

4   Click the volume curve at the beginning of the 6th measure to set a new point at that position.

Let's change the value of the new control point so that it is the same as the default volume level for the track (0.0).

5   Drag the new control point (at the 6th measure) up to the horizontal gray default volume line. The default volume level is 0.0 dB.

The volume of the track gradually changes between the 5th and 6th measures to fade the volume of the track up from silence.

6   Press the Left Arrow key to move the playhead to the beginning of the Hollywood Strings region. Solo the track, then play the first part of the song and listen to the first note in the Hollywood Strings track fade-in.

7   Unsolo the track and play the beginning of the song again to hear the fade-in mixed with the rest of the tracks.

Now that you've added control points to the volume curve for the Hollywood Strings track, let's hide the volume curve.

8   Press A to hide the volume curve on the Hollywood Strings track, then press Return to move the playhead back to the beginning of the timeline.

Notice that the volume slider for the Hollywood Strings track is at the lowest volume position. That's because the volume curve is now at its lowest position, which is at the beginning of the timeline.

9 Try to drag the volume slider on the Hollywood Strings track.

The volume slider is deactivated because the volume curve has been changed. Once you add the first control point, the volume slider is turned off. Each time you click the deactivated volume slider, the volume curve appears to show you why the slide control is off, and to give you the option to work on the track automation curve.

10 Click the volume slider again to hide the track curve if it is showing.

11 Play the beginning of the song. Watch the volume slider in the Hollywood Strings track as the song plays.

The volume slider moves to reflect the value of the volume curve. By setting the control points, you have automated the volume slider.

12 Press Command-S to save your work.

Now that you know how to add control points to dynamically change the volume of an individual track, let's try setting control points on the pan automation curve.

Dynamically Panning a Track

Just as you added control points to the volume curve, so you can add control points to the pan curve to move the sound from one speaker to the other. Let's say that the backup vocalist holding the shaker is pacing back and forth—maybe she had a little too much coffee, or maybe she's just trying to liven things up. Whatever the reason, panning a sound from one speaker to the other is an advanced mixing technique that can add a little excitement to an instrumental part.

Let's add some control points to the pan curve on the Shaker track to give it some dynamic movement within the stereo field.

1   On the Shaker track, click the triangle to reveal the active track curve (either volume or pan).

2   Click the pop-up menu on the left side of the track's automation row and choose Track Pan, if it is not already showing.

3   Drag the control point at the beginning of the pan curve and drag it up to the highest position (–64), which is panned all the way to the left.

> **NOTE ▶** You may have created a new control point at the beginning rather than grabbed the one already there. No worries. Just position the new control point in the desired position. Having two control points near the beginning won't make a difference in this situation.

4   Drag the control point to the lowest position (+63), which is panned all the way to the right.

Zero (0) is the center panning position.

5   At the beginning of the first region in the Shaker track, click the pan curve to add a control point.

6   Hold the Shift key while dragging the control point up to +47, which favors the right speaker but is not panned all the way.

Shift-dragging control points allows you move them precisely to a specific number by showing each incremental number as you drag.

7 Add another control point at about halfway through the first Shaker region. (the beginning of the 11th measure). Set the control point value to –48.

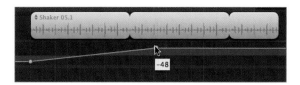

This position in the stereo field is opposite that of the first control point and will favor the left speaker.

8 Set one more control point at the end of the first Shaker region. Make the value of the control point the same as that of the first point (+47).

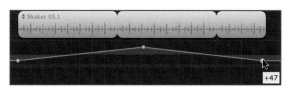

9 Solo the Shaker track and listen to the panned region.

Sounds like someone moving from one side of the stage to the other with the shaker. You have just successfully created a dynamic panning effect.

TIP ▶ You can select multiple control points at once by dragging the pointer along the track automation curve to select the points. You can also select all of the points on a curve by clicking the empty space at the left of the automation row, below the track header. Once the points are selected, you can raise or lower them all at the same time by dragging one of the selected points up or down. To delete selected points, press the Delete key. You can deselect points by clicking the empty space in the track curve.

Project Tasks

Now we'll dynamically pan the second region in the Shaker track.

1 To begin, add three control points (beginning, middle, and end) to the Shaker track's pan curve.

2   Set the three control points so that the sound will pan from one speaker to the other and then back.

> **TIP** ▶ You need to move only the middle control point, since the other two are already in position.

3   Press A, or click the triangle on the Shaker track, to hide the track automation curve. Then unsolo the Shaker track and listen to the song with the dynamically panned shaker.

4   Save your changes as *HB dynamic* to the My GarageBand Projects folder.

Excellent work. Now it's time to move on to the master track.

> **NOTE** ▶ If you didn't complete all of the previous exercises, feel free to open the project **HighwayBoundDYN** to catch up. Save the project to the My GarageBand Projects folder.

Working with the Master Track

Throughout this lesson, you've been mixing the song by adjusting individual tracks. The song has come a long way since the arrangement you started with, and the mix is almost finished.

There's one thing left to work with, and that is the master track. Unlike individual tracks, the master track controls the entire song. In the next series of exercises, you'll work with the master track to change the volume and effects for the overall song.

There are two ways to show the master track:

▶   Choose Track > Show Master Track.

▶   Press Command-B.

Let's try it now.

1   Choose Track > Show Master Track.

The master track appears at the bottom of the timeline. The master track's volume curve appears by default.

2   Click the master track header to select it, if it is not already selected.

The master track header appears purple.

The master track's pop-up menu lets you show either the master volume curve or the master pitch curve. You can set control points on the master pitch curve to dynamically change the pitch of (transpose) the overall song.

Understanding the Volume Controls

There are four volume controls to consider as you finish your song. Each volume control adjusts a particular level.

Track Volume

Track volume is the volume level of an individual track. You adjust it using either the track's volume slider or the track's volume curve. The purpose of adjusting the track volume is to make it higher or lower in the overall mix so you can balance the levels of the different tracks.

Master Track Volume

To dynamically adjust the volume level of the overall song, you adjust the volume of the master track, which is a combination of all the mixed individual tracks. To change the master track's volume, you adjust the control points in the master track volume curve. The time to adjust the master track volume is after you have balanced the levels of all the individual tracks.

Master Output Volume

It's important to understand the difference between the overall song volume, which you control through the master track, and the master output volume. The *master output volume* is the volume level that goes out of GarageBand to the computer. This output level determines the level your song will have when it is exported—for example, when it is output from GarageBand to iTunes.

You can control the master output volume of the song by using the master volume slider, located in the lower-right corner of the window.

This slider should be adjusted only after you have mixed the levels of the individual tracks and then adjusted the master track volume. Once the overall song is mixed, you use the master volume slider to raise or lower the output level. This step ensures that you avoid clipping and that the export volume of the finished song is not too high or too low. You'll adjust the master volume slider in Lesson 8 when you learn to export and share projects.

Computer Output Volume

The computer output volume is how loud you hear your GarageBand project through your headphones or computer speakers. You should always use the volume controls for your computer to adjust the loudness in your headphones and speakers. You should not use the master volume slider in GarageBand for this purpose. Adjusting your computer's output volume level lets you listen to your GarageBand music as loudly or quietly as you like without changing the output level of the actual project so that it exports too loudly or too quietly.

> **NOTE** ▶ You can adjust the volume for your computer via the volume slider (speaker icon) in the menu bar at the top of the screen, the volume control keys on the computer keyboard, or the Sound pane of your System Preferences window.

Now that you understand the different volume controls, let's focus on the master track volume and the master output volume.

Fading Out the Master Track

One of the most important features of the master track is that it can be used to dynamically change the volume curve of the overall song. You can easily add control points to the master volume curve, just as you would to any other track. Instead, for this exercise, you'll use a handy fade-out feature.

1 Move the playhead to the beginning of the 29th measure and play the end of the song to hear how it sounds.

Did you notice that the strings keep going long after the last bass note? Let's fade out the master track after the last note in the Electric Bass track.

2 Choose Track > Fade Out.

Four control points appear at the end of the song to gradually fade out the ending. The last control point ends at the same time as the end of the longest region in the timeline.

3 Play the end of the song and listen to the master track volume fade out at the end.

Now the song has a nice clean fade after the last note. You can always adjust the fade control points as needed.

4 Press Command-S to save your progress.

Testing Your Trained Ear

Now that you know how to mix a song in GarageBand, let's put your ear to the test. In this exercise, you'll listen to the original unmixed song, then the mixed song. See if you hear the difference in the two versions.

1 Open the project **HighwayBoundUnmxd** to hear the original unmixed version of the song.

2 Play the first half of the song.

3 Choose File > Open Recent > **HighwayBoundFX** to open your finished mix. If you didn't complete all of the mixing steps, you can open
   HighwayBoundFinal from the Lesson_06 folder.

4 Play the finished mix.

   As the song plays, ask yourself the following questions:

   ▶ Does the mixed version of the song sound better than the unmixed
   version?

   ▶ Do you notice the left-to-right placement of the different tracks in the
   stereo field?

   ▶ Do you notice the overall balance of the volume among the tracks?

   ▶ Can you hear that the lead instruments (guitars) are louder in the mix
   than the supporting instruments?

   If you heard any or all of these things, you've trained your ear to hear
   beyond the basic song.

Congratulations! Now you know how to mix your songs to make them sound
professional. Before moving on to the next lesson, one other element of mixing and arranging is good to know.

Ducking Background Tracks

The last mixing feature you'll explore in this lesson is the new ducking feature.
Ducking was designed for easy mixing of your podcasts and movie sound-
tracks, so you'll work more extensively with it in Lesson 7. However, this is
a good time to introduce you to ducking, since it can also be used to automatically lower (duck) the levels of backing tracks to favor the levels of other
tracks.

You apply ducking by setting which tracks are lead tracks and which are backing (background) tracks. Whenever there is sound on the lead tracks, the volume of the backing track is lowered. Tracks that aren't designated as lead or
backing stay the same.

The term *duck* comes from the shape that a volume automation curve would take if you had to lower the volume of a track every time a part played, or a voice spoke, on another track. The volume curve would look as if it were ducking (bending down) out of the way of the waveform in the other track.

The best part of the new ducking feature is you don't have to use control points to create the ducking effect.

You can turn on the ducking feature by pressing Command-Shift-R or by choosing Control > Ducking.

1   Open the project **HighwayBoundFinal** if it is not already open. Unlock each of the Drum Kit tracks.

> **NOTE** ▶ If you do not unlock tracks prior to turning on the ducking controls, you will see an alert tells you that they need to be unlocked to make changes.

2   Choose Control > Ducking to turn on the ducking controls in the current project.

A ducking control with arrows pointing up and down appears in each track's header. The control lets you set whether the track is a background track (blue down arrow), is neither a background nor a lead track (gray), or is a lead track, causing other tracks to be ducked (orange up arrow).

The ducking controls in the middle tracks are set so that the lead instrument tracks (Acoustic Guitar 1 and Acoustic Guitar 2) are causing background tracks to duck. The Tambourine and Shaker tracks show blue down arrows in the ducking controls, so both tracks will automatically lower their volume levels whenever sound is playing in the lead instrument tracks. The ducking feature works only while the controls are active.

3 Play the project with the ducking controls active.

Notice that the volume levels of the Shaker and Tambourine tracks stay below the lead instrument tracks, and they rise only in the parts of the song where the lead guitars aren't playing.

The ducking controls are most commonly used for podcasts or for projects with narration so that music levels automatically lower whenever someone is talking.

Project Tasks

This is a good time to practice some of the skills you've learned throughout this lesson. Try changing the effects on the Acoustic Guitar tracks to change the sound. Apply effects to other tracks. Modify the volume levels and pan positions, and add dynamic changes within the track automation curves. Since the master track is showing, you can open the Track Info pane and try different effects on the overall song. You can even record your own parts, or add more loops to enhance the song.

Finally, feel free to experiment with the ducking controls. When you're finished, don't forget to save the project.

Lesson Review

1. What features are included in the track mixer for each track?
2. What happens to a track's level meter if a track's volume is too loud?
3. How do you change where a sound is placed in the stereo field?
4. Where can you add or change effects applied to a track?

5. How do you add or change the effects for the overall song?

6. How do you change the volume or panning of a track over time?

7. How do you add control points to a track's volume or pan automation curve?

8. What track curves are available for the master track?

9. What feature allows you to automatically lower the level of a track based on the sound in another track?

10. Which controls should you use to adjust the volume level in your headphones or speakers while working with GarageBand?

Answers

1. The track mixer includes a volume slider, a pan dial, and a level meter with clipping indicators for each track.

2. The level meter peaks in the red, and the clipping indicators turn red.

3. Change the pan position of a track to move that track to a different location in the left-to-right stereo field.

4. In the Track Info pane.

5. Change the master track settings in the Track Info pane.

6. You can dynamically change the volume or panning of a track over time by adding control points to the volume or pan automation curve.

7. You can add control points to the volume or pan curve by showing the curve and clicking it where you want to add a point.

8. The master track includes a volume curve for dynamically adjusting the volume of the overall song in the timeline. You can also dynamically transpose a song by adding control points to the master pitch curve.

9. The ducking feature automatically lowers the level of background tracks to favor lead tracks based on the settings in the ducking controls.

10. To change the playback volume in your headphones or speakers, use the volume controls for the computer, not the master volume slider.

7

Lesson Files

Time

This lesson takes approximately 90 minutes to complete.

Goals

Create a new podcast episode

Add the Speech Enhancer effect to voice tracks and customize the settings

Import and edit a project within a project

Add artwork to the Media Browser and podcast track

Edit marker regions

Build a title sequence in the podcast track

Crop and resize artwork in the Artwork Editor

Add a URL and a URL title to a marker region

Lesson 7
Creating Podcasts

Podcasts are like radio or TV shows that can be downloaded over the Internet, and they are one of the fastest-growing forms of multimedia. With GarageBand, you can create podcast episodes and then upload them to the Internet using iWeb or another application.

There are four primary types of podcasts: audio podcasts; enhanced audio podcasts with markers, artwork, and URLs; video podcasts containing a movie; and enhanced video podcasts containing a movie, markers, artwork, and URLs.

In this lesson, you'll first learn how to create a new podcast episode and set up the voice tracks for recording. Then you'll work on a real-world enhanced audio podcast with multiple voice tracks, markers, artwork, and URLs. Along the way, you'll build an opening title sequence, learn how to add a project to another project, and edit marker regions and artwork.

Creating a New Podcast Project

Many of the projects you've worked on so far were already in progress when you started. Since you'll be creating your own podcasts from scratch once you finish this book, let's take a look at the template for podcast episodes in GarageBand.

1   Open GarageBand. If GarageBand is already open, choose File > New.

2   In the New Project dialog, click the Podcast icon.

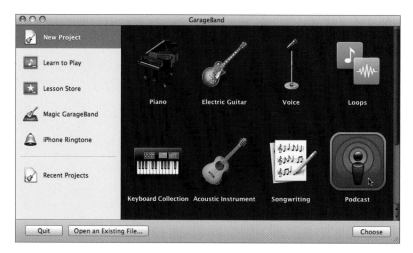

3   Save the project as *Podcast Template* to your My GarageBand Projects folder.

4 Click Create.

Podcast track

Editor   Media browser

A podcast project opens. The podcast track is empty, the editor has marker information, and the Media Browser is already showing. The Media Browser contains Audio, Photos, and Movies buttons for the three types of media files, a Source list where you can navigate to the media files you want to use, and a media list showing the media files in their current location.

Notice that the Photos button and the iPhoto icon in the Media Browser are selected. If the iPhoto library on your computer includes movie files, they will appear in the lower pane of the Media Browser whenever you select the iPhoto icon. Any files in the Photos pane of the Media Browser can be used as episode artwork for your podcast.

You can also add other folders of still images and photos to the Photos pane, so you can access artwork files anywhere on your computer.

Showing and Hiding the Podcast Track, Browser, and Editor

Because you created a podcast project using the template from the New Project dialog, all of the basic tracks and panes are already showing. However, as you work on your podcast project, chances are you'll need to show and hide different tracks and panes as needed to maximize your timeline workspace. Many of these elements use the same shortcuts you'd use if you were working on a music project.

1   Choose Control > Hide Editor, or press Command-E, to hide the editor.

2   Choose Control > Hide Media Browser, or press Command-R, to hide the Media Browser.

The podcast template includes a podcast track and prebuilt audio tracks, including Male Voice, Female Voice, and Jingles. You can always add more tracks or delete unneeded tracks from the timeline. Also, the ducking controls are on and have the voice tracks set as lead tracks; the Jingles track is set as a backing track that will be ducked as needed to favor the voice tracks.

3   Choose Track > Hide Podcast Track, or press Command-Shift-B.

You generally won't hide the podcast track while you're working. In fact, you're more likely to want to show the podcast track in a project you may not have originally designated as a podcast.

4   Choose Track > Show Podcast Track, or press Command-Shift-B.

The podcast track reappears along with the Track Info pane for the selected track (in the screen shot above, the podcast track has been selected).

5   Click the Preview button (the square on the right side of the podcast track header) to open the Podcast Preview window.

The Podcast Preview window—which is similar to the Movie Preview window—allows you to see the podcast's artwork as you play the project.

Now that you are comfortable with showing and hiding the various panes you'll be using during this lesson, let's move on to setting up your podcast recording equipment.

> **NOTE ▶** A project can include either a podcast track or a movie track, but not both. If you try to show the video track for a project that contains a podcast track, a dialog appears asking if you want to replace the podcast track with a video track, and vice versa.

Choosing Podcast Recording Equipment

Recording audio for a podcast in GarageBand can be as simple or as complicated as needed for your particular project. For example, if your podcast needs only one voice track, you can record the narration to an enabled Real Instrument track by connecting a microphone to your computer or by using your Mac's built-in microphone (if it has one). An iSight camera will also work because it includes a fully functioning microphone that is perfect for recording podcast audio. In fact, you can even record remote interviews with iChat users.

Remember that the voice tracks you record for a podcast are Real Instrument tracks, so they follow the same recording rules you learned in Lesson 3. With an approved audio interface, you can record a maximum of eight Real Instrument tracks and one Software Instrument track simultaneously. Without an audio interface you can record only one stereo track, or two mono tracks at the same time.

Due to the popularity of GarageBand, a variety of third-party recording equipment is available. When I'm creating projects for these books, I try to find equipment that is both GarageBand-friendly and modestly priced.

The podcast you'll be working on later in this lesson includes two Real Instrument voice tracks, plus three additional Real Instrument tracks used for the ongoing podcast music.

To record my narration, I used the new Blue Snowball USB microphone, which plugs into any USB port. It doesn't require any additional software or drivers, and it works well for these types of projects.

For more complex podcasts with multiple voice tracks being recorded simultaneously, I use the Edirol FA-101 interface, which has ten inputs and ten ouputs.

Many audio devices will work for recording multiple tracks. You may also want to set up a Software Instrument track and an external MIDI or USB MIDI keyboard to trigger sound effects—as you did in Lesson 4—during your podcast.

I also used the M-Audio iControl for GarageBand controller, which I have to confess I've been using throughout the process of writing this book.

The iControl is a GarageBand-specific USB device that allows you to select, mute, solo, record enable, pan, and adjust volume on tracks, as well as operate the transport controls, add effects, and adjust the master volume.

For me, using the external iControl device to control the tracks and transport controls, and an external MIDI keyboard to trigger sounds, enables me to focus on the live podcast interviews without using the mouse or computer keyboard.

Again, let me stress that none of this equipment is necessary to create a podcast, and you can often get along with minimal equipment. I just wanted you to be aware of some other options, especially if you plan to create a lot of enhanced podcast episodes or music projects.

Before recording, make sure that your equipment is turned on and properly connected to the computer. For more specifics on the operation of your equipment, refer to the equipment manuals.

Exploring the Vocal Track Presets

GarageBand includes microphone settings and vocal enhancement effects that can be applied to a vocal track before or after recording. These effects—available in the Track Info pane—are designed to improve the quality of your vocal recordings.

1   In the timeline, double-click the Male Voice track header.

The Track Info pane appears for the selected track. Notice that the Vocals instrument category has been selected, and Male Basic is the specific preset. This default setup works fine for basic vocal recording, but let's take a look at the podcast-specific vocal presets.

2 In the Track Info pane, select Podcasting in the instrument category.

There are 12 presets from which to choose, including five Male and five Female Voice presets: iSight Microphone Male, Male Narrator Noisy, Male Narrator, Male Radio Noisy, Male Radio, iSight Microphone Female, Female Narrator Noisy, Female Narrator, Female Radio Noisy, and Female Radio.

The presets that have *Noisy* in the title include automatic noise reduction to help eliminate unwanted background noise in the recording.

The iChat and iSight presets are designed specifically for tracks using those methods of recording.

3 Select the Male Narrator preset.

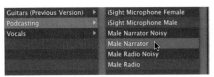 

The preset effect changes, and the track header's name changes to reflect the new preset.

4   In the Track Info pane, click the Edit tab to reveal the effects details.

You can see that the preset includes two effects that have been applied: Bass Reduction and a Speech Enhancer effect set to Male Narrator.

The effects settings for the Speech Enhancer also let you choose which type of microphone you are using. This is very useful for enhancing the quality of recordings if you are using a built-in microphone.

5   To open the Speech Enhancer presets, roll over the rectangle graphic (it looks like a microphone for this effect). This is the Edit button. When an overlay appears with sliders, click the Edit button for the Male Narrator preset.

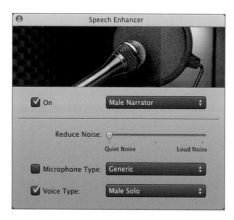

The Speech Enhancer's Preset window includes a preset pop-up menu, which will automatically change to Manual if you modify any of the current settings. There is also a Reduce Noise slider, which is currently at the lowest setting. In the Microphone Type menu, you can choose the type of microphone, and in the Voice Type menu, you can select the type of voice.

6   Click to select the Microphone Type box, then click the Microphone Type menu to see the choices, ranging from PowerBook G4 Titanium to iMac G5 with iSight. Choose the microphone type that best fits your recording situation. Choose Generic if you are using an external microphone.

7   Choose a preset from the menu at the top of the Speech Enhancer's Preset window. Try a preset that best suits the type of recording you might use in a podcast. If you're unsure, try Male Narrator or Female Narrator.

A dialog appears, showing that you've made changes to the current instrument settings.

8   Click Save As on the dialog to save the track instrument settings. Name the preset *My Podcast Voice*, and click Save.

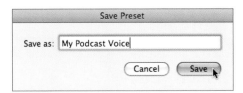

9   In the Speech Enhancer's Preset window, choose your new preset from the menu. Then close the window to add your custom settings to the selected track.

NOTE ▶ Once you've made changes to a track's preset vocal effect, you may want to change the name of the track to reflect the current effects. The track name automatically changes if you use a standard preset.

Project Tasks

If you have a microphone attached to your computer, take a moment and try recording to the track you just set up. Remember the shortcuts R to start recording and Spacebar to pause. Also make sure that the track you want to record is selected and the Record Enable button is turned on. Record a little narration about yourself, or your family, or read a few paragraphs from this book. The important thing is the practice, not the content of the recording. When you've finished, save and close the project.

Adding the Speech Enhancer Effect to Recorded Vocal Tracks

Now that you know how to create a new podcast project and set up your vocal tracks, let's fast-forward to a podcast project that is a little further along. In this exercise, you'll apply the Reduce Noise control to a voice track. Along the way, you'll also use many of the skills you've learned so far.

1   Open the project **PodcastStart** in the Lesson_07 folder and save it to your My GarageBand Projects folder.

The project contains a lot of media files and is fairly large, so it may take a few minutes to save.

This podcast project is an interview with film producer Kim Dawson about an exciting new high-tech educational project he is involved in, called TEQGames. The podcast is episode 15 of the podcast series InVision Digital Showcase, which features professionals and industry leaders in film, television, and multimedia production. It includes three recorded Real Instrument voice tracks, and two Jingles tracks containing royalty-free Jingles that came with the GarageBand Apple Loops. The podcast track has been hidden so you can focus on the recorded tracks first.

Notice that the ducking controls are on, and that the recorded voice tracks are the priority (lead) tracks. The music and effects tracks are ducking (lowering their volume) to favor the priority tracks.

NOTE ▶ Since the podcast is basically a recorded conversation, the LCD is set to the Time mode rather than the Measures mode as in the projects you worked with in previous lessons.

2   On the LCD, click the seconds (00) numerals and drag upward until they read 35.000 (35 seconds) in the time display. This is right before Kim speaks for the first time.

3   Press C to turn on the cycle region, and create a yellow cycle region from the beginning of the Kim Dawson region to around 2:00.

The exact length of the cycle region is not important. The idea is to isolate a portion of his dialogue so that you can evaluate it as you work with the noise-reduction feature.

4   Double-click the Kim Dawson track header to open the Track Info pane for the track. Then click the Edit tab to see the track's details.

The track has the Speech Enhancer effect applied, with the Male Narrator preset.

5   Click the Edit button to open the Speech Enhancer's Preset window.

6   Press the Spacebar to begin playback of the cycle region.

7   Press S to solo the selected track.

You can hear a bit of air conditioner room noise when Kim speaks. You may not be able to get rid of all the noise, but you can certainly reduce it.

8   Continue playback and drag the Reduce Noise slider from the lowest setting (Quiet Noise) to the highest setting (Loud Noise). Feel free to choose a setting in between that you like better.

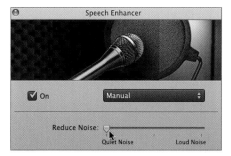

Can you hear the difference in the noise while he's talking? Did you notice that moving the slider all the way to the right reduces the noise but also diminishes the sound of his voice? Since vocals trump noise in a podcast, move the slider back to around –26.

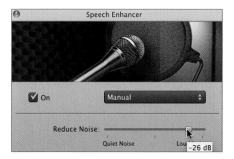

9   Close the Speech Enhancer's Preset window and pause playback.

10   Press S to unsolo the Kim Dawson track, then press C to turn off the cycle region.

> **NOTE** ▶ Normally, when you choose a new preset in the Track Info pane, the name of the track also changes. Podcast tracks are commonly named after their subjects or contents. If you have manually named a track, the name will stay with the track when you make changes in the Edit pane.

As you can see, it is easy to apply the Speech Enhancer effect to a track before or after it has been recorded.

Importing a GarageBand Project

If you have listened to the beginning of the podcast, you'll notice that it's pretty darn boring without any music. Not to mention that it's just a voice without any visuals, which you'll also fix shortly. First, let's add the official podcast jingle to the beginning and end of the project. You could choose from one of the many professional jingles included with GarageBand in the loop browser. However, since this is a real podcast series, you'll be using the official podcast theme that was created in GarageBand.

When you create a piece of music in GarageBand, you could mix and export the finished song, then import it into the podcast project, or simply import the GarageBand project. That's right: You can import a project into another project. If you save a project with iLife preview, you can preview and use it in any of the other iLife applications, including GarageBand.

Saving a Project with iLife Preview

In this exercise, you'll open the project **IDSPodcastTheme** and save it with iLife preview. If you've been following the exercises in the book, you've been instructed to click No when prompted to save projects with iLife preview. It takes longer to save projects with iLife preview, and the feature is only for the projects you want to share with other iLife applications—or GarageBand itself. So this is the first time you've needed that feature.

1   Save the current project (click No if asked to save with iLife preview). Then choose File > Open and select **IDSPodcastTheme** from the Lesson_07 folder.

2   Play the project once to familiarize yourself with another example of a piece of music created from scratch in GarageBand using primarily Apple Loops.

    You've come a long way since the beginning of this book, and you have the skills to build this song or your own original composition.

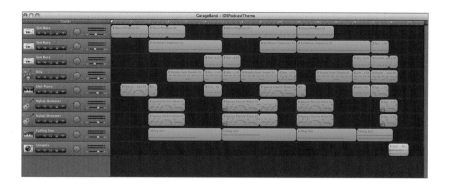

3 Choose GarageBand > Preferences. In the Preferences window, click the General button.

4 At the bottom of the General preferences, select the Audio Preview option, if it is not already selected.

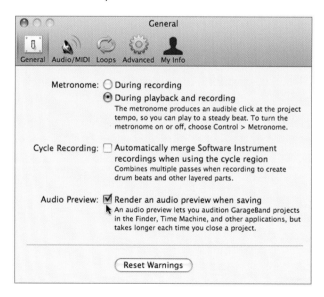

NOTE ▶ If you turn on this feature, an alert about saving with iLife preview will appear when you save other GarageBand projects until you turn it off again. When the feature is on, saving each project will take longer. You can always go back to General preferences and turn off iLife preview as needed.

5   Close the Preferences window.

Since this project needs to be available in the Media Browser, let's go ahead and change the location while saving with iLife preview.

6   Choose File > Save As. Select the Music folder in the Finder sidebar, then click the GarageBand folder. Click Save.

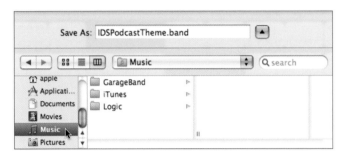

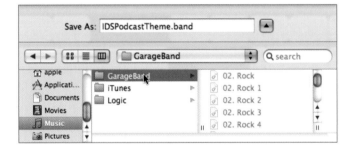

TIP▶ In your home folder (User), the /Music/GarageBand/ folder is the default location for saving GarageBand projects. If you want to make all of your projects easier to locate and use in other applications, start saving to the default location (once you finish this book).

7   Choose File > Close. Click Yes if prompted to save with iLife preview.

This project now includes a rendered preview of the project, so you can preview it in other iLife applications.

Adding a GarageBand Project from the Media Browser

To use a GarageBand project in another project, you need to place it in the Media Browser. In the previous exercise you saved the **IDSPodcastTheme** project to the /Music/GarageBand folder, so it should now be ready add to your project. Saving the project with iLife preview means that you can add it to your GarageBand timeline. By default, the Media Browser gives you access to your iTunes library in the Audio pane of the Media Browser. You can also add other folders containing audio files, including GarageBand projects. Let's reopen the **PodcastStart** project and show the Media Browser.

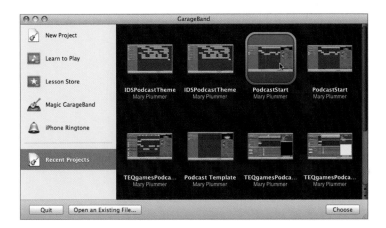

1 Click Recent Projects in the New Project dialog, or Choose File > Open Recent and select the **PodcastStart** project you were working on earlier in this lesson.

> **NOTE ▶** Your recent projects list will look different from the screenshot because mine includes multiple versions of the same projects that I needed to create for the book lessons.

2 Press Command-R to show the Media Browser. Click the Audio button to show the Audio pane within the browser.

Your iTunes folder and default GarageBand folder are automatically showing in the Audio pane.

NOTE ► The Media Browser in the screen shot includes some files that you won't have in your browser because I have the World Music Jam Pack installed on my computer, as well as additional music projects that are not part of this book.

3   In the Media Browser, select the GarageBand folder, then double-click the **IDSPodcastTheme** in the lower pane to preview it.

NOTE ► Normal GarageBand project file icons look like a document (paper) with a guitar printed on it. GarageBand project files saved with iLife preview show only a guitar icon.

4   Drag the **IDSPodcastTheme** project from the Media Browser to the empty space below the Jingles track in the timeline.

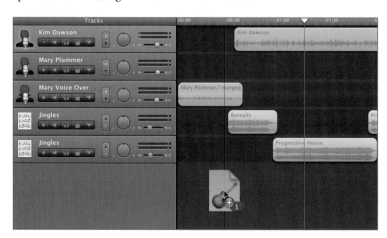

The project file appears in the timeline as an orange Real Instrument region. The small guitar icon in the upper-left corner of the region shows that it is a GarageBand project instead of a normal audio file.

5   In the timeline, move the region in the IDSPodcastTheme track so that it starts at the beginning of the project.

6   Play the first part of the project to hear the **IDSPodcastTheme** project as the intro music for the podcast.

Notice that the ducking controls are working as they should and are automatically ducking (lowering) the volume level of the Jingles track to give volume priority to the narration track.

7   Press Command-S to save your progress.

8   If you see a dialog asking if you'd like to save the project with iLife preview, click No.

There is no reason to save this project with iLife preview at this time.

You've successfully added a GarageBand project to the timeline of another project. Of course, you might wonder what the big deal is about that. You can also export a finished mix of a song and just add the mixed audio file to a project the same way. Well, what if you change your mind? More importantly, what if your clients change their mind? It happens more often than not, depending on the client. What if someone wants you to make changes to the song in the timeline? If it's an audio file, you have to find the original project, or re-create it, then make the changes and export it again, then add the exported mix to the project. On the other hand, if you have a project in the timeline, you simply open the project in the editor, click the Open Original Project button, and *voilà*! You're working on the original song again. Best of all, when you save the changes, the project automatically updates in the timeline. It sounds more complicated than it is. Let's just try it.

Editing a GarageBand Project Within Another Project

To demonstrate editing a project within a project, you're going to open the **IDSPodcastTheme** project from the **PodcastStart** project, change the panning on several tracks, then save it so it automatically updates in the **PodcastStart** project.

1   In the timeline, select the orange (imported) **IDSPodcastTheme** project. Then press Command-E to open the editor.

2   In the editor, click the Open Original Project button (looks like a document with an arrow) to open the original song project.

A dialog appears asking if you want to close the current project and open the other.

3   Click Open Original Project.

NOTE ▶ If another dialog appears, prompting you to save the changes with iLife preview, click No.

The original **IDSPodcastTheme** project opens.

4   Pan the Elec Piano track two dots to the left (10 o'clock position).

5   Pan both Nylon Shimmer tracks two dots to the right (2 o'clock position).

6   Press Command-S to save the changes to the project.

7   Press Command-W to close the current project. If prompted, click Yes to save with iLife preview.

The **PodcastStart** project automatically reopens. A dialog appears asking if you want to update the changes to the IDSPodcastTheme region.

8   Click Update Region to update the project within the current project.

The project updates, and the **PodcastStart** project automatically saves. You've just witnessed a very advanced maneuver made easy—GarageBand-style.

NOTE ▶ If you choose not to apply the changes when you return to the project you started from, the link between it and the imported project is permanently broken. Also, extending the length of the imported project can result in regions being deleted when you apply the changes to the project it is imported into.

There's just one more thing to do: Add the **IDSPodcastTheme** song to the end of the project. No problem. You'll just copy the file and paste it at the end of the project.

9   Hide the editor if it is showing. Select the **IDSPodcastTheme** project at the beginning of the timeline and choose Edit > Copy, or press Command-C. Then move the playhead to 00:06:10 (end of the Kim Dawson region) in the timeline.

10   Make sure the IDSPodcastTheme track is selected, then choose Edit > Paste, or press Command-V to paste the project at the playhead position.

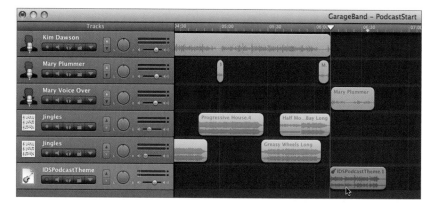

11   Play the end of the project to hear the **IDSPodcastTheme** song with the rest of the tracks.

Excellent! The song works well at both the beginning and end of the project.

Now that the audio tracks are in place, including the theme song at the beginning and end of the project, it's time to add some artwork.

Working with Artwork and Markers

The next step in building the podcast is to enhance it with artwork and markers. When you add episode artwork to a podcast, the artwork appears when you play the podcast episode in iTunes and when you work with it in iWeb.

Artwork added to the podcast track creates a marker region the same length as the artwork in the podcast track. Marker regions are used in podcasts to literally *mark* a specific region in the timeline to include artwork, a chapter title, or a URL. When you publish your podcast, iWeb or other software will use these marker regions to include the designated information for that region in the project.

You can edit, move, and resize marker regions anytime while creating your podcast project. You can also add chapter title markers and URL markers to the podcast track and edit them. In addition to the artwork used as marker regions in the podcast track, you can also designate the episode artwork in the editor. The episode artwork appears in the Podcast Preview window whenever there is no artwork for the current marker region.

> **NOTE** ▶ If you didn't complete all of the previous exercises, feel free to open the project **PodcastMusic** to catch up.

Adding Artwork to the Media Browser

The artwork you'll be using for this project is in the GarageBand09_Book_Files folder on your desktop. You can add artwork folders to the Media Browser in the same way you added your projects folder earlier in this lesson. The difference is that you need to place podcast artwork in the Photos pane of the Media Browser.

1   Open the Media Browser, if it is not already showing. Then, in the Media Browser, click the Photos button to show the Photos pane.

If you recall, this is the default Media Browser pane when you create a new podcast project in GarageBand.

2   In the Dock, click the Finder icon to open the Finder window.

3   In the Finder, locate the GarageBand09_Book_Files folder on your computer's desktop (or other location where you installed it).

4   In the GarageBand09_Book_Files folder, open the Lesson_07 folder and select the PicturesforPodcast folder. Drag it to the Photos pane of the Media Browser, then close the Finder window.

The PicturesforPodcast folder appears in the browser.

5   Click the triangle at the left of the PicturesforPodcast folder to view the folder's contents, if they are not already showing.

You'll see that it contains three folders: Interview Pics, InVision Digital
Showcase Titles, and TEQGameswebpics.

6   Click the timeline and press Return to move the playhead to the beginning
of the project, if it is not already there.

7   Choose Track > Show Podcast Track.

The podcast track appears at the top of the timeline, above the other
tracks. The podcast track is where you can view and edit marker regions
for a podcast episode.

8   Click the rectangle Preview button in the podcast track header to show the
Podcast Preview window.

Now you can see the artwork in the Podcast Preview window as the project plays.

Adding Episode Artwork to the Project

Episode artwork represents the entire project—like a movie poster or CD
cover. People will see it when they choose your podcast to download or preview. The project can have only one piece of episode artwork. Let's take a
moment and assign a file as the episode artwork for this podcast.

1   Press Command-E to show the editor.

The editor appears for the podcast track. The Episode Artwork well on the
side of the editor is currently empty. The marker area of the editor shows
the marker regions and artwork already added to the podcast track.

The Podcast Preview window shows that no artwork is available because the playhead is at the beginning of the project, where there is no artwork in the podcast track.

2   If necessary, press Command-R to show the Media Browser.

3   In the upper pane of the Media Browser, select the InVision Digital Showcase Titles folder located inside the PicturesforPodcast folder.

These titles were created in Motion. You can create title stills in virtually any graphics program, such as the iWork applications. As long as the files are QuickTime-compatible, you'll be able to include them as podcast artwork.

TIP ▶ Double-click a file in the Media Browser to see a larger version in the lower pane. Click the image again to return to the file list.

4   Select the file **IDSPodcast 01** and drag it to the Episode Artwork well in the editor.

The episode artwork appears in the editor. The episode artwork also appears in the Podcast Preview window because there is no other artwork in the playhead position of the podcast track.

What if you change your mind after you've added episode artwork? You can drag the artwork from the well, and it will vanish in a puff of smoke— really. Or just drag another piece of artwork to the well to replace the original.

5   Drag the episode artwork out of the well and release the mouse.

Poof—the well is empty again. You'll add another piece of artwork later in the lesson. You'll also learn to crop and resize artwork images as needed.

Adding Artwork to the Podcast Track

Since you already have the titles showing in the Media Browser, let's go ahead and build the opening title sequence and create marker regions as we go. The opening title sequence will include images that go with the **IDSPodcastTheme** song and intro voiceover for the podcast. Let's zoom in to the timeline for a larger view of the podcast track as you add the artwork.

1   Press Command-E to hide the editor.

    Notice the empty space in the first 35 seconds of the podcast track. You'll fill that space momentarily with a marker region.

2   Press Control–Right Arrow several times until the ruler shows 10-second increments instead of 30-second increments. (The timeline's zoom slider should be around one-third of the way across the slider control.)

3   Click the empty space at the beginning of the podcast track to deselect all of the marker regions within that track.

    If marker regions are selected when you add new artwork to the podcast track, the new artwork may replace the first selected marker region, instead of creating a new marker region.

    If you add artwork to the beginning of an empty space in the podcast track, it will automatically fill the space.

4   Drag the **IDSPodcast 01** file from the Media Browser to the empty space at the beginning of the podcast track in the timeline and release the mouse.

The new marker region fills the empty space from the place where you released the mouse to the next marker region. Don't worry if it doesn't start exactly at the beginning of the timeline. We'll fix that easily in a moment.

5   Drag the left edge of the new marker region in the podcast track until it extends to the beginning of the timeline.

6   Move the playhead over the first marker region, if it isn't already there, to see the artwork in the Podcast Preview window.

Hmm. The artwork is all right, but the title doesn't fit very well in the Podcast Preview window and some of the words are cut off.

Let's go ahead and edit the artwork before adding additional titles.

Working with the Artwork Editor

GarageBand includes a handy Artwork Editor you can use to resize and crop your artwork to show all or part of the original image. To access the Artwork Editor, double-click the Artwork box in the Artwork column of the editor.

1   Select the podcast track header and open the editor, if it is not already showing.

The podcast editor displays information about each marker and has an Add Marker button to create new markers. You'll explore the podcast editor features over the next few exercises. For now, let's focus on the Artwork column, which shows a thumbnail picture of each marker's artwork in order from top to bottom.

2   Double-click the Artwork box for the first marker (at the top of the list).

The Artwork Editor opens with the artwork. The square frame represents what will be displayed in your podcast.

3   Drag the size slider all the way to the left so that the title graphic touches the left and right edges of the square frame.

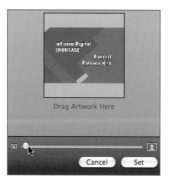

4   Click the Set button to set the changes to the image and close the Artwork Editor.

NOTE ▶ To crop an image in the Artwork Editor, you need to drag the zoom slider toward the right to zoom in on the image, then drag the image area within the square to reposition the image.

The episode artwork updates according to the changes you made in the Artwork Editor.

Building a Marker Title Sequence

Many traditional podcasts show a few images to introduce new people or subjects, but for the most part the artwork is literally as visually interesting as a piece of art on a wall that you look at as you listen to a radio talk show. There's nothing wrong with that. Some art is better than no art, but if you have the additional stills and titles, why not use them? GarageBand makes it so easy to add markers to keep the podcast visually stimulating.

There are two ways to add markers, and essentially artwork, to the podcast:

▶ Move the playhead to the position where you'd like to add a marker and click the Add Marker button in the podcast editor.

▶ Drag a piece of artwork to the podcast track and release it where you'd like to add the marker.

In this exercise you'll use both methods. Since you've already used the second method, let's start with the button method.

When you add a new piece of artwork, it won't replace the entire existing artwork. Instead, it will split the original and replace the marker region from the position you release the artwork to the next marker region.

1   Play the project from the beginning and pause the playhead when the narrator says "I'm your host…" (the 00:09 mark).

2   Press the Left Arrow key to move the playhead 1 second earlier (00:08).

3   In the podcast editor, click the Add Marker button.

A new marker appears in the markers list, and the long marker in the podcast track splits at the playhead. This marker does not contain any artwork. No problem; it's easy to add artwork later. Let's go ahead and add two more markers for the titles.

4   Add two more markers with the Add Marker button at 00:11 and 00:13.

For the last marker you'll move the playhead, then drag a piece of artwork to the playhead position to create the marker.

5   Move the playhead to 00:27.

6   Drag **IDSPodcast 07** from the Media Browser to the playhead position in the podcast track.

> **TIP** Dragging an artwork file over the playhead on the podcast track hides the dark gray vertical alignment guide that you can use for precision placement. Instead, drag a file just below the podcast track so that you can see the guide.

The previous marker region splits in two, with the artwork-free region first and the IDSPodcast 07 region second.

To add artwork to the empty markers, simply drag the desired artwork from the Media Browser to the Artwork column and drop it into the Artwork box for the specific marker. The Artwork box is easy to find: It's the light gray square labeled "Drag Artwork here."

7 Drag the **IDSPodcast 05** file from the Media Browser to the Artwork box for the second marker.

8 Drag the **IDSPodcast 02** file from the Media Browser to the Artwork box for the third marker.

9 Drag the **IDSPodcast 03** file from the Media Browser to the Artwork box for the fourth marker.

All of the show titles artwork is in place. Let's take a look before moving on to the next section.

10 Play the first part of the project and watch the titles change in the Podcast Preview window.

Great work, except all of the titles need to be resized in the Artwork Editor.

Project Tasks

Take a minute and use the Artwork Editor to fix the artwork in the title sequence. You already resized the artwork in the first marker. Double-click each of the artwork thumbnails for the remaining titles and resize them so the left and right edges touch the boundaries of the visible area in the Podcast Preview window. Don't forget to click the Set button once you've resized the image. When you're finished, save your progress. This whole process should take only about minute or so. The edited artwork thumbnails will all show white bars at the top and bottom of the image.

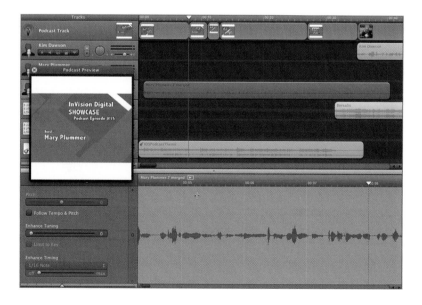

NOTE ▶ If you didn't complete all of the previous exercises, feel free to open the project **PodcastMarkers** to catch up.

Editing Marker Regions

Your goal in this exercise is to change the timing of the second marker region to match the narration. The first thing you need to do is find the narrator's waveform and visually identify when she says, "I'm your host…" That's where the second marker should begin. For this maneuver, you'll look at the voice region in the editor.

1   Select the region at the beginning of the Mary Voice Over track to view it in the editor. If the editor is not currently showing, double-click the region to show the editor.

2   Click the Playhead Lock button in the lower-right corner of the timeline so that it looks like two playheads on top of each other, rather than in separate positions.

Playheads unlocked   Playheads locked
(out of sync)   (in sync)

This way, the two playheads will move together rather than independently. By default, once the locked playheads in both the timeline and the editor reach the center of the timeline, they will remain there while the project scrolls behind them.

3   Press Return to move the playheads (timeline and editor) to the beginning of the project.

4   Drag the editor zoom slider to around the halfway position for a clear view of the waveforms within the region.

5   Play the project from the beginning and pause when you hear the voice-over say, "I'm your host" (around 09.45).

The playhead is somewhere over the spoken words "I'm your host." Look for the silent section of the waveform (a flat horizontal line) right before the "I'm your host" waveform area. That silence is where you need to move the playhead and, essentially, where you'll want to start the second marker.

6   Move the editor playhead to the end of the silent space before the voice-over line "I'm your host" (00:09.000).

This ought to be perfect. You could manually drag the playhead farther to the left over the silent area, but it's always a good idea to work with whole seconds whenever possible to keep things simple.

Now that you know when you want the second marker to start, you can manually drag it in the podcast track, or give it a new starting timecode in the podcast editor. For this exercise, you'll change the timecode in the editor.

7   In the podcast track, click the marker region beneath the timeline playhead.

The editor changes to the podcast editor, with the second marker selected in the markers list.

8   In the Time column, change the time for the second marker from 08.000 to 09.000.

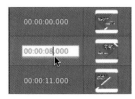 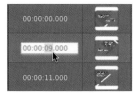

The beginning of the second marker region moves to 00:09. However, this leaves a 1-second gap between the first and second marker regions.

9   In the podcast track, drag the right edge of the first marker region toward the right until it ends at the 00:09 mark.

NOTE ▶ You could have achieved the same result by simply extending the first marker region. The advantage to setting a marker's time in the editor is that you have precision control of the starting point of a marker.

Good job. You've completed the title sequence.

Viewing Additional Marker Information

In addition to the Time and Artwork columns, the podcast editor also includes chapter title, URL title, and URL for each marker.

1   Select the podcast track header in the timeline to select the podcast track.

Notice that all of the marker regions appear white (selected) in the timeline, and all of the markers are also selected in the podcast editor.

2   Click any empty space in the timeline below the podcast track to deselect all of the markers.

The podcast track remains selected until you select another track header or a region in the timeline.

In the podcast editor the marker regions are listed in chronological order from the beginning of the project. Notice the columns from left to right: Time, Artwork, Chapter Title, URL Title, and URL for each marker. You may have to scroll right to see all of the columns.

3   Drag the vertical scroller to scroll down through all of the project's markers.

As you can see, there is a title sequence at the end of the project similar to the one at the beginning. The end title sequence markers include URL information for the InVision Digital Showcase website that produced the podcast. You'll add URL information for the TEQGames website in the next exercise.

The checkboxes in the editor show how the marker will be designated. Adding artwork to a marker region automatically selects the Displays Artwork checkbox for that marker.

Adding a URL to a Marker

You can add a URL (website address) to a marker region in a podcast or a marker in a movie and view the URL when you play the movie or podcast in iTunes. Not only will viewers see the URL when they play the finished project, but they can also click the URL onscreen to open the webpage in their browsers.

If you add a URL title, the title appears in the Album Artwork window of iTunes (in a published podcast), and clicking it opens the webpage for the URL. An example of a URL title might be "For More Information," or "Check out our website."

Let's add a URL title and link to the middle of the project where the guest
gives the web address orally. You'll add the URL to an existing marker region.
To get there, you can navigate in the timeline or simply double-click the
marker in the editor.

1   In the editor, scroll to around the middle of the markers in the list and
     locate the marker that begins at 00:02:58.500. Then double-click any blank
     area on the marker's row in the marker list to jump the playhead to the
     marker's location in the timeline.

You can now see the selected marker's artwork in the Podcast Preview
window. The selected marker region is also selected (white) in the podcast track.

2   Press the Spacebar to play the project from the playhead position and listen to the dialogue that goes with the selected marker.

You can clearly hear the guest Kim Dawson giving the web address for the TEQGames website as well as describing what it looks like when you get there. This is a prime opportunity to add a URL title and link to the podcast.

3   For the selected marker in the editor, click the URL Title field. Type *click here to visit TEQGames.com* and press Return.

This message will appear below the podcast artwork once the podcast is published, or played in iTunes.

4   For the selected marker, click the URL field. Type *TEQGames.com* and press Return.

GarageBand will automatically add the *http://* to the address.

Notice that Display URL is selected after you add a URL to the marker.

Once you add a URL, the URL title for that marker appears over the marker artwork in the Podcast Preview window to show that the marker includes a URL. Don't worry if it looks like the URL title is in the middle of the artwork; it will actually show up below the artwork in the exported podcast.

5   Play the marker to see the URL title appear in the Podcast Preview window.

Feel free to click the URL title in the Podcast Preview window to open the webpage. If your computer is not currently connected to the Internet, your browser will try to open the page and then tell you that you're not connected.

Project Tasks

The URL title and link you added work great. But the title is not onscreen very long. Since the next two marker regions also show the front page of the TEQGames website, it would be nice if the link extended through all three marker regions. To accomplish this and give viewers enough time to see and click the URL, let's add the same information to the next two markers as well.

Select each of the two marker regions after the one you just modified, and add the same URL title and URL as you did in the previous region. You can retype the information in each field, or copy and paste the information from a field in one marker to the same field in another. When you are finished, save your progress.

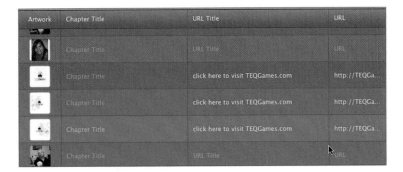

Using Marker Artwork for Episode Artwork

While you are in the editor, this is a good time to pick a new image for the episode artwork. Earlier you used the title of the show, but it didn't really say much about the content. Instead, let's choose one of the pictures of the band to use as the episode artwork. You could look through all of the images in the Media Browser or simply drag one of the images from the Artwork column in the editor to the Episode Artwork well.

1   In the editor, locate the marker that starts at 00:00:13.000.

2   Select the artwork image for the marker and drag it to the Episode Artwork well.

It's that easy. Of course, if you look at the Artwork column, the marker that you borrowed the episode artwork from may no longer contain artwork. No problem. You can simply drag the episode artwork to the empty Artwork box for that marker.

3 If necessary, drag the episode artwork from the well to the empty Artwork box in the Artwork column.

NOTE ▶ If you accidentally erased the episode artwork by dragging it somewhere other than the empty box in the Artwork column, just choose Edit > Undo and try again.

Mission accomplished. The enhanced podcast is complete, including the URL links that you just added.

Adding Episode Info to a Podcast

The last step needed to complete your podcast episode is to add the episode information, which includes the title, artist information, a description of the episode, and a parental advisory. The episode information is available when you work on the podcast in iWeb and when you view the podcast in iTunes.

1 Double-click the podcast track header in the timeline.

The podcast track appears in the Track Info pane.

2   Click the Title field and type *InVision Digital Showcase Podcast #15.* Press Return.

The Artist and Composer fields will use the default information as designated in the GarageBand preferences. These fields can be modified to reflect the name of the company producing the podcast, or whatever is appropriate for the specific podcast. For this exercise you can leave those fields with the default information.

3   From the Parental Advisory menu, choose Clean.

4   Click the Description area and type *An interview with film producer Kim Dawson about TEQGames.*

The description could be more in-depth if you'd like. You might include additional names, references, or information that would be useful in finding this podcast.

5   Choose File > Save As and save the finished podcast as *PodcastFinal* to the My GarageBand Projects folder.

6   Play the podcast from start to finish to see the completed project.

All of the artwork images are included in the folder that you added to the Media Browser if you want to change or edit some of the images.

NOTE ▸ If you didn't complete all of the steps in this lesson and would like to see the finished version of the podcast, open the project **PodcastFinal** from the Lesson_07 folder.

You've added many of the advanced podcast features to this project and have a good working knowledge of how to build your own podcasts. Once you have created a podcast episode, you can send it to iWeb to publish it to the Internet. You'll learn more specifics on exporting and sharing your finished podcast in Lesson 8.

Lesson Review

1. How do you create a new podcast using the Podcast template?
2. Where can you add and adjust the Speech Enhancer effect for a voice track?
3. What must you do to a project so that it can be previewed or added to another project?
4. In what two locations can you add artwork to a podcast?
5. How do you crop or resize artwork in a podcast project?
6. Where do you add URL titles or URL information to a marker region?
7. Where do you edit the podcast episode information?

Answers

1. You open a template for a podcast episode from the New Project dialog.
2. In the Track Info pane, click the Edit tab, then click the Edit button for the Speech Enhancer effect to open the effect's Preset window and modify the effects settings on the selected track.
3. You must save a project with iLife preview in order to preview it in the Media Browser and use it in another project.
4. You can add artwork to a podcast as a marker region in the podcast track and marker information in the podcast editor.
5. You crop or resize podcast artwork by double-clicking the artwork in the editor and modifying it in the Artwork Editor.

6. You add URL titles or URL information to a marker region in the podcast editor.

7. You edit a podcast episode's information in the Track Info pane for the podcast track.

8

Lesson Files

GarageBand09_Book_Files > Lesson_08 > RootsRockMixedFX

GarageBand09_Book_Files > Lesson_08 > Alaska Sunrise

GarageBand09_Book_Files > Lesson_08 > PodcastFinal

GarageBand09_Book_Files > Lesson_08 > TouchPetsScoreFinal

Time

This lesson takes approximately 45 minutes to complete.

Goals

Prepare a project for iTunes

Evaluate a song's output

Share a finished song with iTunes

Explore sharing projects with other iLife applications

Sharing Your Finished Projects

Now that you know the basics of how to record, arrange, and mix your projects in GarageBand, it's time to learn how to share them with other iLife applications and export them to iTunes, where they can be downloaded to your iPod or burned to a CD.

All of the iLife '09 applications are designed to work together seamlessly. You can write music in GarageBand and export your songs to iTunes; score your iMovie video and export it as a QuickTime movie or send it to iDVD; send your finished podcast to iWeb to publish on the Internet; or create a whole playlist of original songs to be shared with any of your applications.

The focus of this lesson is learning how to export your GarageBand projects to other iLife applications.

Sharing with Other iLife Applications

If you haven't experienced the ease of working across multiple iLife applications, you will do so as you explore the various means of sharing GarageBand projects. The key to this integration is the Media Browser, which is accessible from both iLife and iWork (as well as from many other applications).

Sharing your projects with other iLife applications involves two simple steps. First, you save your project. Then, you simply choose Share from the main menu and then one of the following menu commands:

▶ Send Song to iTunes—This command places a mixed copy of the track into your iTunes library. We'll explore this option fully in the next section.

▶ Send Ringtone to iTunes—You used this in Lesson 5.

▶ Send Podcast to iWeb—You'll explore this option later in the lesson.

▶ Send Movie to iDVD—You'll explore this option later in the lesson. If you don't have a video track, this option is dimmed.

▶ Export Song to Disk—This option guides you through saving an MP3 or AAC file to a hard disk.

▶ Burn Song to CD—This option allows you to record a song directly on an audio CD.

Exporting Projects to iTunes

Exporting to iTunes is as simple as choosing Share > Send Song to iTunes. Before you begin exporting, however, you'll need to do a few things to prepare your songs.

In the next series of exercises, you'll set your GarageBand preferences to create a playlist in iTunes. Then you'll evaluate a song to make sure that you're exporting the whole song, and you'll check the output level for clipping. Finally, you'll export your song to a new playlist in iTunes.

Because you'll be working with a finished, mixed song, this is a great time to practice your ear for music so that you can hear beyond the basics.

Setting Preferences for iTunes

To prepare a song to export to iTunes, the first step is to set your song and playlist information in the Export pane of the GarageBand preferences. For

these exercises, you'll continue to use the RootsRock song that you worked
with in Lesson 6, "Mixing Music and Effects."

1   Open the project **RootsRockMixedFX** from the Lesson_08 folder.

2   Choose GarageBand > Preferences to open the Preferences window.

3   Click the My Info button to open the My Info Preferences pane, if it's not
    already showing.

    Next, you'll need to name the iTunes playlist, composer, and album. By
    default, GarageBand names the playlist and album after the registered user
    of the computer.

4   Type *GarageBand '09* in the iTunes Playlist field. Type your name in the
    Artist Name and Composer Name fields. Type *GarageBand '09 Book
    Album* in the Album Name field.

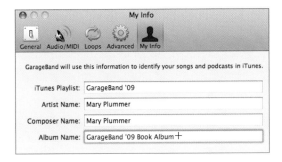

5   Click the Advanced button and make sure that the Auto Normalize check-
    box is selected.

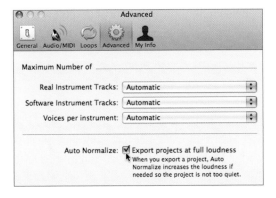

The Auto Normalize feature is great for exporting songs to iTunes because it will automatically adjust the volume level to make sure that it's loud enough.

NOTE ▶ Although Auto Normalize is good for exporting music to iTunes, you don't always want to use it. If you're scoring video with dynamic music and sound effects that have very specific volume settings, for example, you probably want to keep the low volume levels when you export the file.

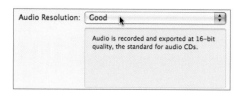

6   Set the Audio Resolution menu to Good, if it's not already at that setting.

The Audio Resolution menu offers three choices: Good, Better, and Best.

▶   Good—The audio is recorded and exported at 16-bit quality, the standard for audio CDs.

▶   Better—The audio is recorded at 24-bit quality for higher fidelity and exported at 16-bit quality. Choosing this will take approximately 50 percent more disk space for recording.

▶   Best—The audio is both recorded and exported at 24-bit quality for the highest audio fidelity. Choosing this will also take approximately 50 percent more disk space for recording and exporting.

TIP ▶ Leave the Audio Resolution setting to Good whenever you are just experimenting with music or recording simple projects or podcasts that will be compressed for CD or web distribution. The Better and Best settings use a lot of disk space and it can add up quickly. If you're laying down tracks as masters for music publishing or other high-end recording, then change the setting when you start the project.

7   Close the Preferences window.

Now that you've set up the export information, iTunes will automatically create a playlist titled iLife '09 Lessons and include the other information in the playlist.

Evaluating a Song's Output Level

It's time to check the output level for the song to make sure it isn't clipping. Remember, the master volume level meter is located in the lower-right corner of the GarageBand window. You can use the master volume slider to raise or lower the output level as needed.

Also, because training your ears takes practice, remember to listen beyond the basic song: Check the left-to-right placement of the various instruments in the stereo field, as well as the balance between the volume levels of the different tracks.

Let's play the song and check the output level. If the level is too high, you'll need to lower the output. If the level is too low, you'll need to raise the output.

1   Press Return and then the Spacebar to begin playback. As the song plays, watch the master volume level meter for signs of clipping.

> **NOTE** ▶ If you don't see the master level meter along the bottom of the GarageBand window, increase the size of the window. You may need to change the resolution of your display to make more room. You can also hide the Track Info pane if it's visible.

If you see any clipping (red) in the meter, stop playback. If you aren't sure if you saw red, the handy clipping indicators (red dots) at the end of the meter light up to let you know that clipping did indeed happen.

You should discover red indicators and some clipping throughout the song.

2   Drag the master volume slider to –2.7 dB to lower the output volume and avoid clipping.

3   Play the song again from the beginning and check the new output level in the meter.

Be careful not to set your level too low. Ideally, your level should peak between the highest green and yellow portions of the meter. Fortunately, you selected Auto Normalize in the GarageBand preferences, so the level should still output with plenty of volume for iTunes.

TIP ▶ If a song sounds as though it ends abruptly, you can choose Track > Fade Out to add a fade to the master track's volume. For more info on fading out a track, check out Lesson 6, "Mixing Music and Effects."

4   Choose File > Save As, and save the project to the My GarageBand Projects folder on your desktop. If you already have a version of the song saved at that location, feel free to overwrite it with this version, which has a corrected master output volume level.

Sending a Song to iTunes

When you export a song to iTunes, the entire song is exported, from the beginning of the first measure to the end of the last region. (If a cycle region is active, only the portion of the timeline included in the region is exported.) But, remember, if you mute or solo tracks, only those tracks set to play will be exported. Let's export the song to iTunes.

1   Choose Share > Send Song to iTunes to export the song.

2   The Share dialog opens and offers several choices.

You can choose to modify the playlist information. You can also select the Compress checkbox, and then choose compression settings from the Compress Using and Audio Settings pop-up menus. If you don't select Compress, GarageBand will create a CD-quality AIFF file.

NOTE ▶ Uncompressed GarageBand projects can be sent to iTunes in AIFF (Audio Interchange File Format) at 44.1 kHz (kilohertz). This is a CD-ready format so that your songs can then be burned to an audio CD. You can also change the file type so that the file can be downloaded to an iPod, or converted to another format, such as MP3, from within iTunes.

3   Click Share.

GarageBand begins creating a mixdown of your song.

During the mixdown process, all of the tracks are mixed (at their current levels) into one stereo pair (left and right) for iTunes.

A progress indicator shows the progress of the mixdown. You can cancel the export process during mixdown by clicking Cancel.

When the mixdown is complete, iTunes opens with your song in the new playlist, and the song automatically plays in iTunes.

4   Press the Spacebar to stop playing the song, then press Command-Q to quit iTunes.

Once your song has been sent to iTunes, you can access it from any of the iLife applications through the Media Browser.

5 Select the GarageBand window to make it active, if it's not already active, and press Command-R to show the Media Browser. Select the Audio pane, if it's not already showing.

The GarageBand '09 Lessons playlist appears in the iTunes library of the Media Browser.

Your song can now be used in any of the iLife applications, including GarageBand and iMovie.

6 Save your project. If necessary, when asked if you'd like to save with iLife preview, click Yes. Then close the project.

> **NOTE** ▶ Any tracks that are muted at the time you export will not be included in the song. This can work to your advantage if you want to make a practice version without certain instruments in the mix.

Enjoy the song. Technically, this composition was crafted by Magic GarageBand Jam, but the settings on your computer will be ready for the next song that you create in GarageBand.

If you would like to export individual tracks from a song, perhaps for a musician to practice with, see "Exporting Selected Tracks" in the appendix, "Bonus Lessons and Materials."

Exporting a Project as a QuickTime Movie

GarageBand projects that contain a movie file can be exported as QuickTime movies. A QuickTime movie exported from a GarageBand project includes both the video and the soundtrack you created. The Movie Sound track that includes the audio that came with the original movie file is also included in the soundtrack unless that track is muted when you export the movie. Let's export a project called **Alaska Sunrise** as a QuickTime movie.

1 Open the project **Alaska Sunrise** from the Lesson_08 folder.

2 Click the Preview button on the right side of the video track header to show the Movie Preview window.

3   Once the Movie Preview window opens, drag the lower-right corner of the window to make it larger (resize it to your own liking).

Since you aren't currently working on the soundtrack, you might as well make the Movie Preview window larger so you can get a good look at the show. This larger preview will also come in handy in the next section when you add markers to the video track before sending it to iDVD.

4   Play the project once through to familiarize yourself with the movie and the score.

This is an example of a more orchestral score. As you can hear, GarageBand is versatile enough for any genre of music.

NOTE ▶ The purple tracks were all recorded as Real Instruments with sounds from my good ol' Roland XP-50 Keyboard with a standard ¼-inch-to-⅛-inch adapter into the computer audio-in port. I used the same keyboard with a MIDI-to-USB cable to record the Grand Piano Angelic Organ tracks so that I could take advantage of the flexible Software Instrument sounds and editing capabilities that come with GarageBand. The Ambience track came from the GarageBand sound effects, and the two Jazz Kit tracks were built from Apple Loops available in the GarageBand loops browser. The Wind Chime region in the Wind Chime track was recorded from the Musical Typing keyboard and a GarageBand Software Instrument wind chime sound.

5 Choose Share > Export Movie to Disk

The Export dialog appears at the top of the screen, with a menu for changing the video settings. You may need to move or resize the Movie Preview window to see the Export dialog.

6 Choose Full Quality from the Video Settings menu.

This setting will maintain the original video resolution and settings. The file size will be only 59.4 MB. Feel free to experiment with the other export settings after you finish the lesson.

The other settings include Email, Web, Web Streaming, iPod, and Apple ( ) TV.

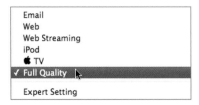

7 Click Export.

The Export to Disk dialog opens to allow you to choose a destination for the file.

8 Save the project to your desktop.

You'll see a series of three progress indicators for creating a mixdown (mixing all of the audio tracks down to a stereo pair), converting files to match export settings, and compressing the movie.

9 When the export is finished, press Command-H to hide GarageBand. Locate the exported file on your desktop.

10 On your desktop, double-click the **Alaska Sunrise** movie file to play it in QuickTime Player.

NOTE ▸ The image is small because that is the image size of the version used in the project. (The original movie was too large to include with the book media.) Feel free to resize QuickTime Player, or press Command-F to see it full screen.

11 Quit QuickTime Player when you are finished.

As you can see, it's incredibly easy to export a scoring project from GarageBand as a QuickTime movie.

Sharing a Project with iDVD

If you have a project containing both video and audio that you'd like to burn to a DVD disc, you can send it to iDVD. When you send a project to iDVD, no compression is applied to the project, because in most cases, you'll want to make those compression changes in iDVD. GarageBand projects that you send to iDVD can use the chapter markers in the project to enable viewers to move to different parts of the movie.

Since you haven't worked with adding markers to the video track yet in this book, now is the perfect time to learn that feature before sharing this project with iDVD.

> **NOTE** ▸ URLs and URL titles will not appear in the finished DVD project.

Adding and Editing Markers

In Lesson 7, you added URL markers to the podcast so that the viewers could see and click a link to the TEQGames website. For this project, you'll add chapter markers to the **Alaska Sunrise** project to identify the wildlife and to mark the appearance of the train. The chapter markers that you add in GarageBand can be used in iDVD. The chapter markers can also be handy for navigating to different parts of the finished movie when you build a soundtrack.

In this exercise, you'll add up to nine chapter markers. True, many of these chapters will be short, but if people watching the DVD want to jump ahead to see a specific animal, they can do so via the corresponding chapter marker.

You can add markers to the video track in the editor.

1 Open the project **Alaska Sunrise** located in the Lesson_08 folder, if it's not already open.

2 Select the video track, then press Command-E to show the editor.

The editor changes to marker view and contains the marker list with columns showing the start time, a still video frame, the chapter title, the URL title, and the URL for each marker.

3   Click the Preview button in the video track header to open the Movie Preview window if it's not already showing. Feel free to move and resize the Movie Preview window as needed to see the editor.

You could set the markers in precise locations. However, for this project, it might be more fun to try adding markers "on the fly"—while the project is playing.

4   Press Return to move the playhead to the beginning.

5   In the editor, click the Add Marker button to add a marker at the playhead position.

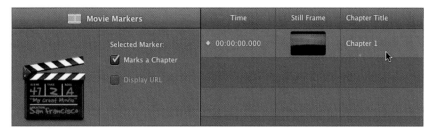

The first marker appears in the marker list. Also, the location on the time-line where you added the marker appears in the Time column, and the frame of the video at that position appears in the Still Frame column.

NOTE ▸ If the beginning of the video clip fades in from black, the still frame for the first marker will also be black.

6   Click the Chapter Title text field and type *Sunrise*, then press Return.

Naming the chapter marker in the Chapter Title field automatically designates the marker as a chapter marker. If you want to name a marker without making it a chapter marker, you can deselect the "Marks a Chapter" option. When would you make a marker and not name it? You'd do so if you were using the marker to identify something—such as where to add a sound effect—to help you create the score or to make a change to the music.

NOTE ▶ To delete a marker, select it in the marker list and press the Delete key.

Now it's time to add the other markers. Don't worry if the position isn't perfect; this is just an exercise.

7   Play the project and click the Add Marker button each time you see a new animal. Also add a marker the first time that you see the train.

Relax. You have more than 30 seconds before the first animal appears. Set markers for the following:

▶   Otter

▶   Whales (tails in water—you won't see an actual whale)

▶   Train

▶   Elk Herd

▶   Dog (optional)

▶   Elk

▶   Bison

▶   Moose

New markers appear in the list to correspond to each click of the Add Marker button.

8   Pause playback when you are finished.

All that is left to finish the markers is to name them and tweak the position if needed.

9   In the marker list, select the Chapter Title field for each marker and type the corresponding animal name. If you don't have all the markers, just name the ones that you do have. The markers in order are Sunrise, Otter, Whales, Train, Elk Herd, Dog, Elk, Bison, and Moose.

To tweak the location, simply double-click the marker's still frame, and the playhead will jump to that location in the timeline. You can then move the playhead a few frames earlier to find the starting location and type the correct timecode (from the LCD) into the marker's Time field.

Let's try one, just to make sure that you know how easy this will be in the future for your own projects.

10   Double-click the still frame for the Otter marker to see the starting frame in the Movie Preview window.

Notice a corresponding yellow diamond (marker) in the timeline. You should also see a new thumbnail showing the marker's still frame with each new marker in the video track.

11 Drag the playhead toward the left to scrub through the video until you see the beginning of the otter scene in the Movie Preview window. (The otter scene begins with a dissolve from the mountains so, technically, it starts while you still see mountains onscreen.)

12 In the marker list, select the Time field for the Otter marker and change the timecode to match the LCD timecode (around 31.852). Select the seconds portion of the time in the Time field and change it first, then adjust the fractions of a second.

The still frame updates to show the new marker frame, and the marker moves to the new location in the timeline.

13 Press Command-S to save your progress.

Chapter markers that you create in GarageBand will be recognized when you play the movie in iTunes, iDVD, or QuickTime Player.

Project Tasks

If you'd like to take a moment and add markers or tweak the still frames for the markers, feel free to go ahead and do so at this time. When you're finished, save your work. Now it's time to send the project to iDVD.

Sending a Movie to iDVD

Once a movie score is finished in GarageBand, sending it to iDVD is only a click away.

1 Make sure that the **Alaska Sunrise** project is open.

2 Choose Share > Send Movie to iDVD.

You'll see a series of progress indicators as the project is prepared for iDVD.

When the export is complete, iDVD will automatically open, and your project will be included in the selected iDVD theme.

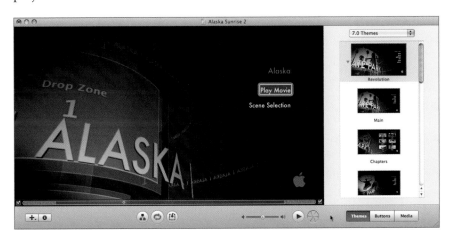

3   Select the Revolution theme from the list on the right side of the window, if it is not already selected. Then click the disclosure triangle, if necessary, to reveal the three standard menus that come with that theme: Main, Chapters, and Extras.

NOTE ▶ If you change themes, you'll see an alert asking if you want to apply the selected theme family to all of the menus in the project. Click OK.

4   Click each of the menu icons (Main, Chapters, and Extras) for the Revolution theme to see the design, and how the chapter markers you created are incorporated into the menu.

5   On the Chapters menu, double-click Scene Selection to see what the chapter scenes will look like on the menu.

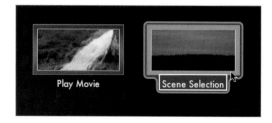

Notice how the Chapters menu shows movie clips named after each of the markers.

NOTE ▶ In this example, the clips playing with each scene in the menu will not always match the chapter title because some of the clips are extremely short. However, if your markers were set at the beginning of each scene, you should see the matching video when you watch the beginning of the menu. You may not see elk in the Elk Herd scene onscreen since the shot was so short in the movie that it finished playing before the scene buttons fully appeared. For most projects, the scenes are much longer, and therefore the clips will match the chapter marker scene names for the duration of the menu.

For this menu, you click the tiny arrows in the lower-right corner to move forward or back to the next set of markers. Each theme handles moving between markers differently.

6   Select the Soft Frame theme to see the Chapters menu in a different theme.

Notice that since the button animation in this theme is quicker, you actually see the Elk Herd at the beginning of the menu.

NOTE ▸ When you change themes, whatever menu you're currently viewing will be the same menu selected in the new theme.

7   Click the Play button to play the template.

The selected menu opens in the iDVD Preview window. You'll also find an onscreen remote that you can use to navigate through the DVD menu just as you would a standard remote control.

8   When you're finished previewing, feel free to close the iDVD Preview window.

9   Quit iDVD. Click Don't Save if you are finished with this example. Click Save if you want to come back and explore this project in iDVD later.

After you quit iDVD, you'll see that the **Alaska Sunrise** project is still open in GarageBand.

10 In GarageBand, choose File > Close.

Once a project is in iDVD, you can change the template, modify the buttons, add images to drop zones, and finish any changes you'd like to make to the project before burning the finished DVD disc.

> **MORE INFO ▶** You can find more information about working with iDVD in the iDVD Help menu, or the book *Apple Training Series: iLife '09.*

Sending a Podcast to iWeb

When you finish your podcast project in GarageBand, you can either send it to iWeb for publishing on the Internet, or you can export it to disk so it can be finished using another application. Compression settings for podcast episodes are available if you choose to export the podcast to disk. Let's open the finished podcast from Lesson 7 and save it to iWeb.

NOTE ▶ Turning on the cycle region has no effect on the length of the exported project. When you export a project containing a podcast track, the entire project from the beginning to the end of the last region is exported.

1   Open the project **PodcastFinal** from the Lesson_08 folder.

2   Choose Share > Send Podcast to iWeb.

     A dialog appears with options for preparing the podcast episode for delivery to iWeb.

3   Choose AAC Encoder from the Compress Using pop-up menu.

     For this podcast, you need to use the AAC format because it is an enhanced podcast with pictures and web links.

4   Choose Higher Quality from the Audio Settings menu to ensure ideal sound for this enhanced podcast.

5   Check to select Publish Podcast, to make sure it is active.

     Deselecting this setting will publish the artwork at the current size, which may not be optimal for podcast publishing.

6   Click Share.

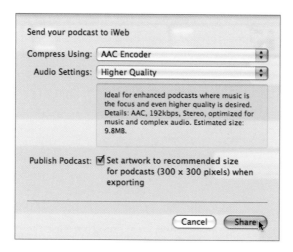

It may take a few minutes for the mixdown and conversion process since the podcast is more than 7 minutes long.

You may see several dialogs on the way to iWeb, depending on how your computer is set up and if you're currently using a .Mac account on your computer. If you don't see one, just move on to the next step.

7   If an iWeb dialog appears asking you to allow or deny information for a keychain, click Allow for this instance.

8   If this is the first time you've opened iWeb, the welcome screen appears. Click Close.

Next you'll be prompted to choose a template for your webpage.

9   Choose Black as the template, and Podcast as the webpage. Then click Choose.

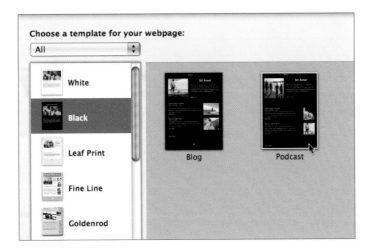

The iWeb page appears with the podcast centered on the page.

10 In the lower-left corner of the podcast player, click the Play button to see the compressed podcast. Feel free to stop previewing the podcast at any time.

11 When you're finished, save your project and quit iWeb.

Once a project is in iWeb, you can change the template, modify the text, and finish any changes you'd like to make to the project before publishing the podcast episode.

12 In GarageBand, close the **PodcastFinal** project.

MORE INFO ▶ You can find more information about working with iWeb in the iWeb Help menu, or the book *Apple Training Series: iLife '09*.

Project Tasks

You've successfully shared three projects with three applications. Now it's your turn to try sharing a project on your own. Open the project **TouchPetsScoreFinal** from the Lesson_08 folder. Play the project once for nostalgia's sake. Then export the movie to disk, or share it with another application. If you feel ambitious, you could add markers to the movie track for each breed when it's singled out. You could also try exporting the PodcastFinal project to iTunes, or to disk to see the different ways to view and distribute a finished podcast episode.

Congratulations! You have completed the sharing lesson and are ready to share, send, and export your own projects.

Lesson Review

1. What should you do to a music project before exporting it to iTunes?
2. What determines the length of the song file exported to iTunes?
3. Where do you set the information for exporting songs to iTunes?
4. What are the two ways that you can export or send a podcast project so that it can be published in iWeb or another application?

Answers

1. Check the master output volume level to make sure the song is at a good level and not too low or too loud (no clipping).
2. The length of a song exported from GarageBand is its duration from the beginning of the first measure in the timeline to the end of the last region in the timeline. If you use a cycle region, only the portion of the timeline included in the region is exported.
3. You can set song and playlist information for iTunes in the GarageBand preferences window.
4. You can either send a podcast to iWeb, or save the project to disk, if you want to export it so that it can be published in iWeb or another application.

Appendix

Bonus Lessons and Materials

This appendix explores a collection of features and advanced techniques that you may find useful in creating your own projects. Each section within this appendix is self-contained, so feel free to step through the ones that interest you, or try them all.

The exercises in this appendix will help you do the following:

Add Loops

Learn how to save your own recordings as loops in the loop browser so that you can index them and use them with other projects.

Edit Real Instrument Loops

Edit and transpose a single bass loop to create a complex bass track for a song.

Export Selected Tracks

Learn how to create different versions of a song, with selected tracks soloed or muted. This technique is perfect for building practice versions for musicians to use for rehearsals, whether at home or on the road.

Minimize Processor Load

Explore some of the options in the GarageBand preferences to help minimize the load on your computer processor. Using these options is ideal if you are working on a slower computer or working with large projects.

Explore Jam Packs

Delve into the exciting Jam Packs available to add new Apple Loops, Software Instruments, sound effects, and more to your library.

Adding Loops and Recordings to the Loop Browser

There is still one sharing technique that you haven't learned yet. This technique involves adding loops to your collections. If you're working with the Jam Pack expansions, you simply install them, and the loops are added automatically to GarageBand so that you can access them in the loop browser. You can also manually add audio files from either the Finder or the timeline to the loop browser.

When you originally installed GarageBand, an index was created for all the Apple Loops included with the program. The loop browser uses this index to find loops and show them in the results list. Adding loops means you'll also be updating the index.

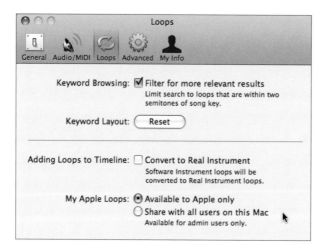

The Loops pane in the Preferences window lets you choose to make your loops available to all users on your computer, or just the current user. Whenever you add loops to your collection through the loop browser, they'll appear in the Library/Audio/User Loops folder in your home folder. The Library/Audio folder is also the default location for Apple Loops and the Apple Loops index.

To add loops, you simply drag the individual loops—or folder of loops—to the loop browser. You can even turn your own recorded regions into loops by dragging them from the timeline to the loop browser.

TIP ▸ When trimming a recorded region to turn it into a loop, make sure that the finished region begins and ends on a beat and starts and ends evenly within measures. For example, the Timpani region in the Loops project starts on the first beat of a measure and ends on the first beat of a measure. If your homemade loops don't start and end with beats and measures, they will slowly lose time with the rest of the song if they are extended to loop repeatedly in the timeline.

Now let's add one loop from the timeline to the loop browser to see how you can turn a recording in the timeline into a loop.

1   Open **LoopSamples** from the Bonus_Projects folder.

The project includes three tracks, each containing a recorded region that can be used as a loop.

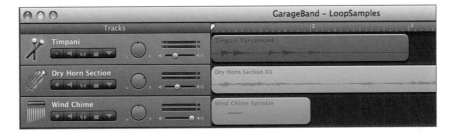

NOTE ▸ These regions were recorded for some of the songs in the lessons and renamed for this exercise.

2   Play the project once to hear the regions. Then open the loop browser (Command-L).

3   Drag the Timpani Turnaround region from the top track in the timeline to the loop browser and release the mouse.

A green circle with a plus sign (+) appears, indicating that you are adding a loop to the loop browser.

When you release the mouse, a dialog appears, asking you to tag the loop with indexing information called *metadata*. Later, when you're trying to find your loop again for another project, you can use loop browser keywords and other search parameters to find it more easily.

4   Use the following figure to select the index metadata for the Timpani Turnaround loop.

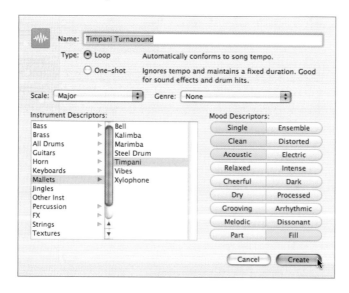

5   Click Create to create the new Timpani Turnaround loop and add it to the loops index.

When it is finished being indexed, your new loop appears in the results list of the loop browser, with the appropriate keyword buttons selected.

6   In the loop browser, click the Reset button to deselect all of the keyword buttons.

Now let's index a one-shot instead of a loop. Loops automatically conform to a project's tempo; one-shots ignore the tempo and maintain a fixed duration. One-shots are files, such as a percussion hit or a sound effect, that are not intended to be looped. For this example, you'll index a Wind Chime region recorded for the **Alaska Sunrise** project.

1   Drag the Wind Chime Sprinkle region from the timeline to the loop browser and release the mouse.

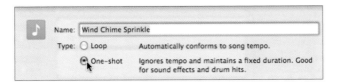

2   In the Metadata dialog, select One-shot as the type of loop. Then select the Mood Descriptors: Single, Clean, Acoustic, Relaxed, Dry, and Fill. Then click Create.

If you're adding a loop from the timeline, the Instrument Descriptors are automatically set to match the track settings for the instrument.

3   In the loop browser, click the Reset button. Then add the Dry Horn Section 01 region to the loop browser. Choose whichever metadata you think is appropriate for the region. Click Create, then Reset once the loop has been indexed.

As you can see, it is quite easy to turn recordings into loops or to add entire folders of loops to your loop browser.

> **NOTE** ▸ You can add loops from other music software to the loop browser. If the loops are not Apple Loops that came with the application, or if they were recorded in the application, they may not appear in the loop browser after they have been indexed. If that is the case, you may need to drag them into a song from the Finder. Loops that are dragged into the timeline from the Finder will not appear in the loop browser. If they don't appear in the loop browser, you can still use them in the timeline. You just won't be able to search for them using the loop browser keyword buttons or columns.

Editing Real Instrument Loops

In Lesson 4, you learned some advanced music arrangement techniques, including editing and transposing Software Instrument loops. In this exercise, you'll edit and transpose the Muted Rock Bass 01 loop to add variety to the bass part and improve the song.

Comparing Bass Parts

First, let's open a revised version of the project and compare the original bass part to the finished one.

1   Open the project **IvoryDreams final** from the Bonus_Projects folder. Play the project once to hear the song created from Apple Loops.

This song uses many of the arranging tricks that you've learned throughout the book. It also contains a complex bass part created from one Real Instrument loop.

2   Close the project and open IvoryDreams bass from the Bonus_Projects folder. Press Command-Shift-S and save the project as **IvoryDreams bass** to your My GarageBand Projects folder.

This project includes only the Real Instrument bass and percussion tracks for the IvoryDreams song. A cycle region has been created over the bass part so the playhead will start at the beginning of the bass part instead of the empty measures at the beginning of the timeline.

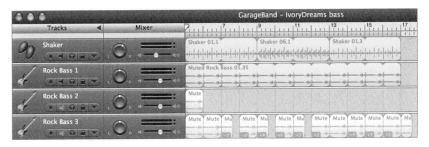

There are three Rock Bass tracks that show the bass part in stages: Rock Bass 1 shows the original bass part with one segment looped over and over; Rock Bass 2 includes one segment of the original loop you'll use to edit and transpose the rest of the track; Rock Bass 3 shows the finished bass track. The second and third bass tracks have been muted.

3   Play the cycle region and listen to the bass part.

It's a cool bass riff, but it's very, very repetitive. Leaving it as is makes it sound incredibly loopy (made from a loop). Editing it will make it sound more like an actual bass part and thus more interesting.

4   Mute the Rock Bass 1 track and unmute Rock Bass 3.

5   Play the cycle region and listen to the finished bass part.

What a difference! Now that you have your incentive, let's go for it.

1   Mute the Rock Bass 3 track and unmute Rock Bass 2.

The first order of business is to duplicate the original Muted Rock Bass 01 loop. Notice you're going to *duplicate*, rather than *loop*. If you extend it so that it loops three times, you'll then have to split it between the segments to make the changes. In this situation, keeping the pieces separate will make them more flexible for editing and transposing. Loops are designed to play seamlessly over and over whether they are looped as one long region or duplicated as a series of repeating loops.

2   Option-drag the region on the Rock Bass 2 track and place the duplicate measure to the right of the original region.

3   Option-drag the new duplicated region and place the duplicate 1 measure to the right.

The original region now appears three times on the Rock Bass 2 track.

4   Press Control–Right Arrow several times to zoom in to the timeline until you clearly see each measure and the 4 beats within each measure.

Next, you'll resize the third region to make it shorter and remove the part of the riff after the first bass note. If you look at the waveform in the bass loop, you'll see there is an initial long note, a short bit of silence (a horizontal line with no waveform), and then another series of notes. Your goal is to cut off the series of bass notes after the initial long note. You can resize Real Instrument loops the same way you resize Software Instrument loops: by dragging the lower-right corner with the resize pointer.

5   Drag the lower-right corner of the third region to the left until the series of notes has been removed. Use the edited region on the track below as a guide for the length.

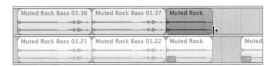

> **NOTE ▶** Real Instrument loops should be resized only from the lower-right corner to maintain the musical timing and pace. You can resize from the left, but in many cases for loops it's better to split the region instead. To trim the front of a loop, you have to split the region and delete the first section. In contrast, Real Instrument *recordings* can be resized from either the lower-right or the lower-left corner, especially if you are editing the region to save as a loop. Also, when you resize a Real Instrument recording, you're resizing it only in the timeline. The region still references the full recording, so it can be resized anytime to reveal the parts of the recording that have been trimmed.

Creating a Loop Pattern

By duplicating and resizing the last region, you have both of the parts needed to create a bass pattern. If you look at the finished bass part on the Rock Bass 3 track, you'll see that the middle section includes one full bass loop, followed by the edited loop. The end of the bass part includes a series of duplicated full loops. For this exercise, you will duplicate, copy, and paste the various parts to create the finished pattern.

1   Press Control–Left Arrow to zoom out one level for a better view of the pattern in the lower bass track.

2 Click the empty space to the right of the edited loop on the Rock Bass 2 track, then select both the middle and last regions in the track.

3 Option-drag the selected regions and place the duplicates at the beginning of the 8th measure.

4 Option-drag the new duplicate regions and place the duplicates at the beginning of the 10th measure. Click the empty space in the track to deselect the regions.

5 Select any of the full loop segments from the track. Choose Edit > Copy, or press Command-C, to copy the loop.

6 Make sure the Rock Bass 2 track is selected. Move the playhead to the 12th measure, then press Command-V or choose Edit > Paste.

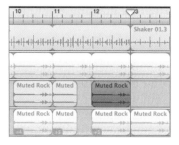

The pasted region appears at the playhead position (bar 12) on the selected track. The playhead automatically moves to the end of the pasted region, so you're in position to paste again.

7 Press Command-V (paste) four more times until there are a total of five consecutive full loop segments in the track.

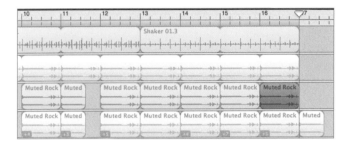

8   Copy one of the resized (shorter) bass loops from earlier in the track and paste it at the beginning of the 17th measure.

9   Press Command-S to save your progress.

Transposing Real Instrument Regions

You can change the pitch of (transpose) a Real Instrument region in the editor the same way you change the pitch of a Software Instrument region. The difference is that you can transpose the region only by one octave (12 semitones) higher or lower. Let's try it.

1   Double-click the resized bass region starting at the 7th measure in the Rock Bass 2 track to show it in the editor.

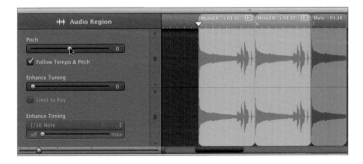

The region pitch controls in the editor transpose only the selected region or regions. In this case, you'll lower the pitch by 7 semitones.

2   Drag the Pitch slider to the left until the field shows −7. You can also type −7 in the field and press Return.

A small –7 appears in the lower-left corner of the transposed region in the timeline to show that the pitch has been lowered by 7 semitones.

3   Play the first three bass regions to hear the original loop followed by the transposed loop.

Project Tasks

You've already completed the bass pattern, and you have transposed a region. Now it's your turn to transpose the other regions in the bass track. Look at the finished Rock Bass 3 track to see how much each bass region needs to be transposed. Keep in mind, some of them don't need to be transposed at all. Play the project once you're finished, and save the project.

Exporting Selected Tracks

Sometimes you want to export only specific tracks. Perhaps you recorded a rough lead vocal track, and you want to practice singing (karaoke-style) to the song without hearing that track. In that case, you would simply mute the vocal track in the timeline and then export the song. Any track that is muted in the timeline will not be exported.

This method works great if you are the lead singer and want to practice your vocals when you're at home, in the car, wherever. You can simply mute the vocal track, export the song to iTunes, and then burn it to a CD or download it to your iPod.

Also, coordinating a time and place to rehearse can be one of the most challenging things for a band. You can use GarageBand to export custom mixes of your original songs so that you can practice even if you can't all be at the same place at the same time.

Let's create three versions of the finished song "Highway Bound" that would be good for rehearsing. Let's assume that the guitar player who plays the Acoustic Guitar 1 track needs some extra practice. To accommodate him, you'll make one version that includes only his part. Then you'll make a second version that includes all of the tracks except for his part so he can practice playing along with the other band members without hearing his guitar part.

Before you export a new version of the song, you'll want to save the project and rename it accordingly.

1 Open the project **HighwayBound** located in the Bonus_Projects folder.

2 Save the project as *HighwayBound Guitar1 only* to your My GarageBand Projects folder.

3 In the Acoustic Guitar 1 track, click the Solo button to solo the track.

The Acoustic Guitar 1 track solos, and all of the other tracks and regions turn gray to indicate they have been muted.

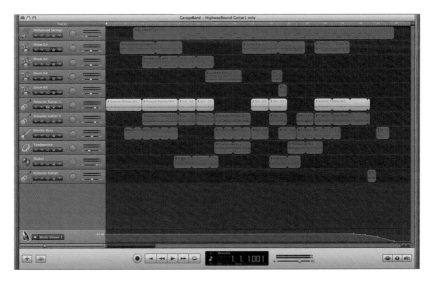

4   Choose Share > Send Song to iTunes to export the guitar-only version of the song.

The new version of the song is exported to iTunes, and iTunes becomes active.

5   Press the Spacebar to pause playback of the song in iTunes, if it is playing.

Now you'll export a version of the song with the Acoustic Guitar 1 track muted.

6   In the Dock, click the GarageBand icon, or press Command-Tab, to switch back to GarageBand.

7   In GarageBand, press Command-Shift-S to open the Save As window. Save the project as *HighwayBound - no Guitar1* to your My GarageBand Projects folder.

8   In the Acoustic Guitar 1 track, click the Mute button to mute the track, which automatically unsolos it. Press Command-S to save the song with the muted track.

This time, the Acoustic Guitar 1 track and regions are gray to indicate they have been muted.

9   Choose Share > Send Song to iTunes to export the version without Acoustic Guitar 1.

The new version of the song is exported to iTunes.

10 Press the Spacebar to pause playback of the song in iTunes, if it is playing.

11 In the Dock, click the GarageBand icon, or press Command-Tab, to switch back to GarageBand.

12 Unmute the Acoustic Guitar 1 track. All tracks should now be active in the timeline.

13 Save the project as *HighwayBound* to the My GarageBand Projects folder. Choose Share > Send Song to iTunes.

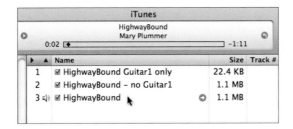

All three versions are now available in iTunes to burn to CD or save to your iPod.

14 Return to GarageBand. In GarageBand, press Command-R to show the Media Browser.

Your playlist is also available in the Media Browser.

As you can see, it is quite easy to send a song to iTunes. When you send songs to iTunes, keep in mind that the exported file will start at the beginning of the project and end when the last region ends in the timeline. If you want to export a shorter version of the song or make it a little longer than the last region, you can use a cycle region. Exporting with a cycle region will export a song the length of the region.

Minimizing Processor Load

Whether you're working with a Mac Pro, Mac mini, iMac, MacBook Pro, or MacBook, it's a good idea to be aware of the features that are the most processor-intensive so you can use them sparingly and thereby get the most out of your GarageBand experience. Certain tracks, for example, demand more from the processor than others:

▶   Software Instrument tracks

▶   Real Instrument tracks using amp simulators

▶   Tracks with a lot of effects

Also, remember that the more tracks you use in a song, the greater the demand on your processor.

If your processor is overloaded, try muting some of the tracks. When you mute a track, it will not be processed. However, soloing tracks, which temporarily mutes unsoloed tracks, does not work the same way. You need to click the actual Mute button on the track.

In the following exercises, you'll learn some additional techniques for minimizing the load that GarageBand places on your computer's processor.

Setting GarageBand Preferences to Help Minimize the Processor Load

Several options in the GarageBand preferences can also help minimize the load on your processor. Let's take a look at some of these options.

1   Choose GarageBand > Preferences to open the Preferences window.

2   Click the Audio/MIDI button to view the Audio/MIDI pane.

3   Check the "Optimize for" section to see which option you have selected.

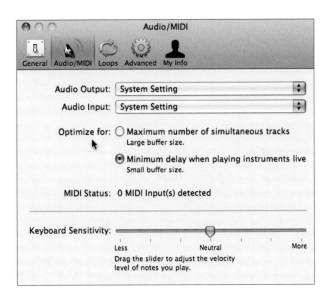

The option "Maximum number of simultaneous tracks" is recommended for slower computers. If your processor is overloading, or the playhead often turns red while playing your song, you may wish to click this option. If you are running a fast computer and haven't had any issues with performance, select "Minimum delay when playing instruments live."

NOTE ▶ The "Minimum delay" option is recommended to help reduce latency (delay) between the time you play your Real Instrument and when you hear the sound. If you have a slower computer, you should use the "Minimum delay" option only while you are recording Real Instrument tracks.

You can also lower the number of tracks and voices per instrument in the Advanced pane of the Preferences window.

4   At the top of the Preferences window, click the Advanced button to view the Advanced pane.

There are three pop-up menus in the Advanced pane. The top two pop-up menus allow you to raise or lower the number of Real Instrument and Software Instrument tracks that you can play in real time.

5   Click the Real Instrument Tracks pop-up menu to see the minimum and maximum number of Real Instrument tracks available.

Notice that the minimum number is 8 and the maximum number is 255.

6   Click the Software Instrument Tracks pop-up to see the minimum and maximum number of Software Instrument tracks available.

Notice that the minimum number is 8 and the maximum number is 64. Software Instrument tracks are more processor-intensive than Real Instrument tracks, so the maximum is lower.

7   Click the "Voices per instrument" pop-up to view the minimum and maximum voices per instrument.

Voices refers to the number of Software Instrument notes that can be played at one time. The more Software Instrument notes (voices) you play at once, the more processor-intensive it is to play that region. The number is different for sampled instruments (including piano, drum, brass, bass, guitar, and woodwind instruments) than for other instruments (organ, electric piano, synthesizers, and clavinet instruments). GarageBand automatically chooses the appropriate number for your computer's CPU. This is the Automatic setting in the pop-up menu.

8   Change all three pop-up menus to Automatic, if they are not already set that way.

If you are having trouble playing your timeline, you can try setting the number of tracks in the pop-up menus to the lowest number. Setting the number of tracks higher than your computer can support can affect your computer's performance.

9 At the top of the Preferences window, click the Loops button to view the Loops pane.

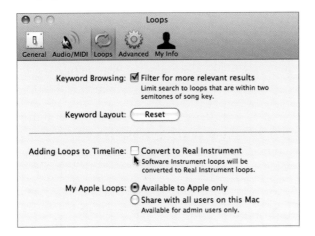

Notice the Adding Loops to Timeline checkbox. If selected, this feature will automatically convert Software Instrument loops to Real Instrument loops when you drag them from the loops browser to the timeline. This feature can be especially handy if you plan on building a song using a lot of Software Instrument loops that don't need editing at the individual note level.

The good news about this feature is that you can turn it off whenever you want to work with Software Instrument loops as-is, then turn it on again when needed.

If you are unsure, leave this option unchecked.

10 Close the Preferences window.

> **MORE INFO** ▸ To find more information about optimizing your system, choose Help > GarageBand Help, then search on *optimizing*. There is a full page of suggestions for optimizing GarageBand performance.

Exploring Jam Packs

If you really enjoy creating music with GarageBand, you can expand your musical horizons with the GarageBand Jam Pack series. These expansion packages of additional song-building elements give you thousands of new ways to enhance your music projects. Literally! Each is loaded with 2,000 to 3,000 new Apple Loops in a wide variety of instruments and genres, plus additional GarageBand Software Instruments, audio effects presets, and new guitar amp settings.

Do you remember the first time you ever got to color with the "big box" of crayons? Not the little 8- or 10-pack, but the big box that had 14 different blues plus colors like burnt sienna, periwinkle, and tangerine. Well, Jam Packs are the musical equivalent of the big box. In fact, the Jam Pack series makes the big crayon box look like a colorful appetizer.

Each Jam Pack in the series is sold separately and includes different musical elements that can be used for GarageBand, Logic, Logic Express, Soundtrack Pro, and any other software that reads AIFF files.

Jam Pack System Requirements

Before installing one of the Jam Packs, you should first make sure that you've installed the software you plan to use with the Jam Packs.

The hardware requirements are 512 MB of RAM (1 GB recommended), plus a DVD drive for installation. Also you'll need from 3.5 to 12 GB of hard disk space for each Jam Pack you install.

Comparing the Different Jam Packs

At the time of this book printing, five Jam Packs are available.

Remix Tools

GarageBand Jam Pack: Remix Tools is for electronic dance music enthusiasts across a number of genres. This Jam Pack includes a wide range of drum machines, beat kits, and authentic vintage beats with actual sounds from the Roland TR-808 and TR-909. There are more than 20 additional beat kits covering genres such as classic, hip-hop, electroclash, house, trance, downtempo, and two-step.

The Remix Tools Jam Pack contains more than 2,000 royalty-free, prerecorded Apple Loops, and it requires 3.5 GB of hard disk space.

Rhythm Section

GarageBand Jam Pack: Rhythm Section provides the core building blocks of drums, percussion, bass, and guitars for rock, jazz, folk, country, and blues musicians. This Jam Pack provides the backing band as you lay down your rhythm tracks. The abundant assortment of basses and guitars covers the most popular studio tones, including Motown sound, 1960s pop, metal, and unplugged rock. There is also a wide range of new software drum kits, including jazz brushes, classic 1970s studio sound, modern rock, plus additional percussion sounds such as congas, bongos, shakers, and steel drums.

The Rhythm Section Jam Pack contains more than 2,000 royalty-free, prerecorded Apple Loops, and it requires 5 GB of hard disk space.

Symphony Orchestra

GarageBand Jam Pack: Symphony Orchestra includes a full orchestral string section: first and second violins, violas, cellos, double basses, harpsichord, and even a Steinway concert grand piano. There's also a wide assortment of brass and woodwinds, including flutes, oboes, French horns, trumpets, trombones, and tubas. You also get an orchestral percussion section that includes timpani, bells, celesta, xylophone, marimba, and more.

The Symphony Orchestra Jam Pack contains more than 2,000 royalty-free, prerecorded Apple Loops, and it requires 10 GB of hard disk space.

Voices

Finding the right backup singers or vocalist for your projects can be a real challenge—especially on a budget. The new Garage Jam Pack: Voices covers all the bases, from soloists to backup singers or an entire choir. Enjoy more than 1,500 Apple Loops featuring professional choirs and soloists in multiple genres and styles. There are also more than 20 software instruments, including voices, choral ensembles, and fantastic drum kits built on the human voice and body.

World Music

GarageBand Jam Pack: World Music places a collection of realistic instruments and loops from around the globe at your fingertips. The exotic string and wind instruments include Indian sitar; Japanese koto; Persian santoor; Highlands bagpipes; and Chinese, Japanese, and Native American flutes, as well as extensive percussion drum kits from Asia, India, the Middle East, Africa, Latin America, and Europe.

The World Music Jam Pack contains more than 3,000 royalty-free, prerecorded Apple Loops, and it requires 12 GB of hard disk space.

Finding Jam Pack Loops and Instruments

Once you've installed one of the Jam Packs, you can access the new instruments, loops, and effects the same way you access the original GarageBand instruments, loops, and effects.

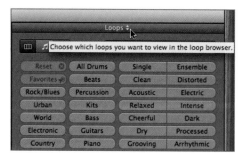

In the Loops menu, you can choose which loops are shown in the loop browser. The menu items are Show All, My Loops, GarageBand, and each of the installed Jam Packs.

The Track Info pane also includes a menu from which you can choose the instruments or effects you'd like to show.

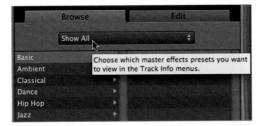

The menu in the Track Info pane for Software Instrument tracks and Real Instrument tracks contains Show All, My Settings, GarageBand, and each of the installed Jam Packs.

Making Jam Pack Loops and Instruments Portable

Be sure to save your projects as an archive (an option in the Save As dialog) if you plan to take a project that includes loops, instruments, or effects from the Jam Packs to a computer that does not have the same Jam Packs installed. Saving the project as an archive includes all of the project's media—including loops, instruments, effects, video, and artwork—in the project.

This saving method makes the file size much larger, but it preserves all of the project's content within the file. This is also a good idea if you plan to back up your final projects to a CD, DVD, or other removable storage medium.

> **MORE INFO ▶** To learn more about the GarageBand Jam Pack series, check out www.apple.com/ilife/garageband/jam-packs.html or visit an Apple store with Jam Packs installed at a GarageBand workstation. Tell them I sent you.

Index

Apple Certification
Fuel your mind.
Reach your potential.

Stand out from the crowd. Differentiate yourself and gain recognition for your expertise by earning Apple Certified Associate certification to validate your iLife '09 skills.

How to Earn Apple Certified Associate Certification

As a special offer to owners of *GarageBand '09,* you are eligible to take the certification exam online for $45 USD. Normally you must pay $65 USD to take the exam in a proctored setting. While this book only partially prepares you for this exam, you can use the free Skills Assessment Guide at training.apple.com/certification/associate to determine if you are ready to take this exam. You may also be interested in *iLife* '09 by Michael E. Cohen, Michael Wohl, Richard Harrington and Mary Plummer. To take the exam, please follow these steps:

1 Log on to ibt.prometric/apple, click Secure Sign-In (uses SSL encryption) and enter your Prometric Prime ID. If you don't have an ID, click First-Time Registration to create one.

2 Click Continue to verify your information.

3 In the Candidate Menu page, click Take Test.

4 Enter GarageEUPP in the Private Tests box and click Submit. The code is case sensitive and are only valid for one use.

5 Click Take This Test, then Continue to skip the voucher and enter your credit card information to pay the $45 USD fee.

6 Click Begin Test at the bottom of the page.

7 When you finish, click End Test. If you do not pass, the results email includes retake instructions. Retakes are also $45.

Reasons to Become an Apple Certified Associate

- **Raise your earning potential.** Studies show that certified professionals can earn more than their non-certified peers.

- **Distinguish yourself from others in your industry.** Proven mastery of an application helps you stand out from the crowd.

- **Display your Apple Certification logo.** Each certification provides a logo to display on business cards, resumes and websites. In addition, you can publish your certifications on Apple's website to connect with schools, clients and employers.

Training Options

Apple's comprehensive curriculum addresses your needs, whether you're an IT or creative professional, educator, or service technician. Hands-on training is available through a worldwide network of Apple Authorized Training Centers (AATCs) or in a self-paced format through the Apple Training Series and Apple Pro Training Series. Learn more about Apple's curriculum and find an AATC near you at training.apple.com.

training.apple.com/certification

Virtual Pets get Social
Only on iPhone and iPod Touch

adventure   care   connect   play

ngmoco:)   App Store Available on the iPhone   touchpets.ngmoco.com

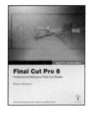